50 Greece Restaurant Dessert Recipes for Home

By: Kelly Johnson

Table of Contents

- Baklava
- Galaktoboureko
- Kadaifi
- Loukoum
- Greek Yogurt with Honey and Nuts
- Kormos
- Revani
- Halva
- Kataifi
- Karpatka
- Bougatsa
- Melomakarona
- Kourabiedes
- Sokolatopita
- Chiboust
- Ekmek Kataifi
- Samosa
- Yiaourti me Meli
- Greek Almond Cake
- Greek Rice Pudding
- Tzatziki Ice Cream
- Greek Donuts (Loukoumades)
- Pita Me Meli
- Kataifi Pie
- Rizogalo
- Greek Walnut Cake
- Melitzana Bougatsa
- Flogeres
- Kavourmas
- Bougatsa with Cream
- Amigdalopita
- Greek Lemon Cake

- Trahanopita
- Sweets of the Greek Gods
- Vasilopita
- Tiramisu Greek Style
- Greek Pumpkin Cake
- Mastiha Ice Cream
- Greek Apricot Preserves
- Almond Halva
- Karpouzopita
- Greek Cheesecake
- Pine Nut Cake
- Chocolate Greek Truffles
- Greek Apple Cake
- Greek Berry Tart
- Greek Fig Cake
- Phyllo Nut Rolls
- Greek Chocolate Soufflé
- Greek Pecan Pie

Baklava

Ingredients:

- **For the Baklava:**
    - 1 package (16 oz) phyllo dough, thawed
    - 2 cups walnuts or pistachios, finely chopped
    - 1 cup unsalted butter, melted
    - 1 teaspoon ground cinnamon
- **For the Syrup:**
    - 1 cup sugar
    - 1 cup water
    - 1/2 cup honey
    - 1 teaspoon vanilla extract
    - 1 teaspoon lemon juice

Instructions:

1. **Prepare the Oven and Pan:**
    - Preheat your oven to 350°F (175°C).
    - Brush a 9x13-inch baking dish with melted butter.
2. **Layer the Phyllo Dough:**
    - Place one sheet of phyllo dough in the prepared pan and brush lightly with melted butter.
    - Repeat layering with about 8-10 sheets, brushing each layer with butter.
3. **Add Nut Mixture:**
    - In a bowl, combine the chopped nuts and ground cinnamon.
    - Sprinkle a thin layer of the nut mixture over the top of the phyllo dough.
4. **Continue Layering:**
    - Add 4-6 more sheets of phyllo dough, each brushed with melted butter.
    - Sprinkle another layer of the nut mixture on top.
    - Repeat this process, ending with about 8-10 sheets of phyllo dough on top, each brushed with butter.
5. **Cut and Bake:**
    - Using a sharp knife, cut the baklava into diamond or square shapes.
    - Bake in the preheated oven for about 45-50 minutes, or until the baklava is golden brown and crisp.
6. **Prepare the Syrup:**
    - While the baklava is baking, combine the sugar, water, honey, vanilla extract, and lemon juice in a saucepan.
    - Bring to a boil, then reduce the heat and simmer for about 10 minutes.
7. **Syrup the Baklava:**

- Once the baklava is baked, remove it from the oven and immediately pour the hot syrup evenly over the hot baklava.
- Allow the baklava to cool completely in the pan; the syrup will soak in and the layers will become sweet and sticky.

8. **Serve:**
    - Once cooled, the baklava is ready to be served. Enjoy!

Feel free to adjust the type of nuts and spices according to your taste!

Galaktoboureko

Ingredients:

- **For the Custard:**
    - 1 cup sugar
    - 1/2 cup semolina (fine or medium)
    - 4 cups milk
    - 4 large eggs
    - 1 teaspoon vanilla extract
    - 1/4 cup unsalted butter, melted
    - 1 tablespoon lemon zest (optional)
- **For the Phyllo:**
    - 1 package (16 oz) phyllo dough, thawed
    - 1 cup unsalted butter, melted (for brushing)
- **For the Syrup:**
    - 1 cup sugar
    - 1 cup water
    - 1/2 cup honey
    - 1 teaspoon vanilla extract
    - 1 teaspoon lemon juice

Instructions:

1. **Prepare the Syrup:**
    - In a saucepan, combine the sugar, water, honey, vanilla extract, and lemon juice.
    - Bring to a boil, then reduce heat and let it simmer for about 10 minutes.
    - Remove from heat and let cool to room temperature.
2. **Make the Custard:**
    - In a saucepan, combine the sugar and semolina.
    - Gradually whisk in the milk, making sure there are no lumps.
    - Place the saucepan over medium heat and cook, stirring constantly, until the mixture starts to thicken.
    - Remove from heat and let cool slightly.
    - Beat the eggs in a separate bowl. Slowly whisk the eggs into the custard mixture.
    - Stir in the vanilla extract and melted butter (and lemon zest if using).
    - Return the saucepan to the heat and cook for an additional 2-3 minutes, stirring constantly, until the custard is thick and smooth.
    - Remove from heat and let cool to room temperature.
3. **Prepare the Phyllo:**
    - Preheat your oven to 350°F (175°C).
    - Brush a 9x13-inch baking dish with melted butter.
    - Place one sheet of phyllo dough in the pan and brush lightly with melted butter.
    - Repeat layering with about 8-10 sheets, brushing each layer with butter.
4. **Assemble the Galaktoboureko:**
    - Pour the cooled custard mixture evenly over the phyllo layers.

- Continue layering phyllo dough on top of the custard, brushing each sheet with melted butter. Use about 8-10 more sheets.
- Brush the top layer with melted butter.
- Using a sharp knife, cut the baklava into diamond or square shapes.

5. **Bake:**
    - Bake in the preheated oven for about 45-50 minutes, or until the phyllo is golden brown and crisp.

6. **Add the Syrup:**
    - Once baked, remove the galaktoboureko from the oven and immediately pour the cooled syrup evenly over the hot pastry.
    - Allow the galaktoboureko to cool completely before serving. The syrup will soak into the layers, giving it a sweet and sticky finish.

Enjoy your homemade galaktoboureko with a cup of coffee or tea!

Kadaifi

Ingredients:

- **For the Kadaifi:**
    - 1 package (16 oz) shredded phyllo dough (kadaifi), thawed
    - 1 cup unsalted butter, melted
    - 2 cups walnuts or pistachios, finely chopped
    - 1 teaspoon ground cinnamon
    - 1 cup sugar
- **For the Syrup:**
    - 1 cup sugar
    - 1 cup water
    - 1/2 cup honey
    - 1 teaspoon vanilla extract
    - 1 teaspoon lemon juice

Instructions:

1. **Prepare the Syrup:**
    - In a saucepan, combine the sugar, water, honey, vanilla extract, and lemon juice.
    - Bring to a boil, then reduce heat and let it simmer for about 10 minutes.
    - Remove from heat and let it cool to room temperature.
2. **Prepare the Nut Filling:**
    - In a bowl, mix the chopped nuts with ground cinnamon.
3. **Assemble the Kadaifi:**
    - Preheat your oven to 350°F (175°C).
    - Brush a 9x13-inch baking dish with melted butter.
    - Gently separate the shredded phyllo dough and place half of it in the prepared baking dish, spreading it evenly and brushing generously with melted butter between layers.
    - Evenly sprinkle the nut mixture over the phyllo dough.
    - Top with the remaining shredded phyllo dough, spreading it evenly and brushing each layer with melted butter.
4. **Bake:**
    - Bake in the preheated oven for about 45-50 minutes, or until the kadaifi is golden brown and crisp.
5. **Add the Syrup:**
    - Once baked, remove the kadaifi from the oven and immediately pour the cooled syrup evenly over the hot dessert.
    - Allow the kadaifi to cool completely in the pan. The syrup will soak into the layers, making the dessert sweet and sticky.

6. **Serve:**
    - Once cooled, cut into squares or diamond shapes and serve.

Enjoy your kadaifi as a delightful dessert after a meal, or as a sweet treat with coffee or tea!

Loukoum

Ingredients:

- **For the Loukoum:**
    - 2 cups granulated sugar
    - 1 cup water
    - 1/2 cup cornstarch
    - 1/4 cup lemon juice
    - 1/2 teaspoon cream of tartar
    - 1 teaspoon rose water or orange blossom water (or a few drops of your favorite flavoring)
    - 1 cup chopped nuts (optional, such as pistachios, walnuts, or hazelnuts)
    - Powdered sugar (for dusting)
    - Cornstarch (for dusting)

Instructions:

1. **Prepare the Pan:**
    - Line an 8x8-inch baking dish with parchment paper or lightly grease it.
    - Dust the bottom and sides of the dish with a mixture of powdered sugar and cornstarch.
2. **Make the Syrup:**
    - In a medium saucepan, combine the granulated sugar and 1 cup of water.
    - Bring to a boil over medium heat, stirring occasionally until the sugar dissolves.
    - Reduce the heat and let it simmer for about 10 minutes.
3. **Prepare the Starch Mixture:**
    - In a separate saucepan, combine 1 cup of water with the cornstarch and cream of tartar.
    - Whisk the mixture over medium heat until it becomes thick and translucent.
4. **Combine the Mixtures:**
    - Gradually pour the hot sugar syrup into the thickened cornstarch mixture, stirring constantly.
    - Continue to cook the mixture over medium-low heat, stirring frequently, for about 30-40 minutes, until it becomes very thick and pulls away from the sides of the pan.
5. **Add Flavoring and Nuts:**
    - Remove the mixture from heat and stir in the rose water or orange blossom water.
    - If using nuts, fold them into the mixture at this point.
6. **Pour into the Pan:**

- Pour the mixture into the prepared baking dish, spreading it evenly with a spatula.
7. **Set and Cut:**
    - Allow the loukoum to cool completely at room temperature. This can take several hours or overnight.
    - Once set, dust the top with a mixture of powdered sugar and cornstarch.
    - Cut the loukoum into small squares or rectangles.
8. **Serve and Store:**
    - Dust each piece with more powdered sugar and cornstarch to prevent sticking.
    - Store in an airtight container at room temperature.

Enjoy your homemade loukoum with a cup of tea or coffee

Greek Yogurt with Honey and Nuts

Ingredients:

- 2 cups Greek yogurt (full-fat or 2%)
- 1/4 cup honey
- 1/4 cup mixed nuts (such as walnuts, almonds, or pistachios), chopped
- Fresh fruit (optional, for garnish, e.g., berries or sliced figs)
- A sprinkle of cinnamon (optional)

Instructions:

1. **Prepare the Nuts:**
   - If desired, toast the nuts lightly in a dry skillet over medium heat for a few minutes until fragrant. Let them cool before chopping.
2. **Assemble the Dish:**
   - Spoon the Greek yogurt into serving bowls or glasses.
3. **Add Honey:**
   - Drizzle the honey evenly over the yogurt.
4. **Top with Nuts:**
   - Sprinkle the chopped nuts over the yogurt and honey.
5. **Garnish (Optional):**
   - Add fresh fruit or a sprinkle of cinnamon if desired for extra flavor and visual appeal.
6. **Serve:**
   - Enjoy immediately, or refrigerate until ready to serve.

This dish is incredibly versatile, so feel free to experiment with different nuts, fruits, or even a sprinkle of granola for added texture. It's a delightful way to enjoy Greek yogurt!

Kormos

Ingredients:

- **For the Kormos:**
    - 1 package (about 200 grams) plain digestive biscuits or Graham crackers, crushed into small pieces
    - 1 cup walnuts or almonds, chopped
    - 1 cup cocoa powder
    - 1 cup powdered sugar
    - 1/2 cup unsalted butter, melted
    - 2 large eggs
    - 1 teaspoon vanilla extract
    - 1/2 cup chopped dried fruit (optional, such as raisins or dried apricots)
    - 1/2 cup dark chocolate chips (optional, for extra richness)
- **For Coating:**
    - 1/2 cup powdered sugar
    - 1/4 cup cocoa powder

Instructions:

1. **Prepare the Mixture:**
    - In a large bowl, combine the crushed biscuits, chopped nuts, cocoa powder, and powdered sugar.
    - In a separate bowl, whisk together the melted butter, eggs, and vanilla extract.
    - Pour the wet ingredients into the dry ingredients and mix until well combined. If using dried fruit or chocolate chips, fold them in at this stage.
2. **Form the Kormos:**
    - Place a large sheet of plastic wrap or parchment paper on a flat surface.
    - Transfer the mixture onto the plastic wrap, shaping it into a log or salami shape.
    - Wrap the plastic wrap tightly around the log and chill in the refrigerator for at least 4 hours or overnight, until firm.
3. **Coat the Kormos:**
    - In a small bowl, mix the powdered sugar and cocoa powder.
    - Once the kormos is firm and set, unwrap it from the plastic wrap.
    - Roll the kormos in the cocoa powder and powdered sugar mixture until evenly coated.
4. **Serve:**
    - Slice the kormos into rounds and serve.

Tips:

- **Texture:** The kormos can be a bit crumbly due to the biscuit pieces. If it feels too dry, you can add a little more melted butter to the mixture before chilling.
- **Flavor Variations:** Feel free to experiment with different types of nuts or add a splash of liqueur for an adult twist.

Enjoy this sweet and satisfying treat with coffee or as a delightful dessert!

Revani

Ingredients:

- **For the Cake:**
    - 1 cup granulated sugar
    - 1 cup semolina
    - 1 cup all-purpose flour
    - 1 cup yogurt (plain or Greek)
    - 1/2 cup unsalted butter, melted
    - 4 large eggs
    - 1 teaspoon baking powder
    - 1 teaspoon vanilla extract
    - 1/2 cup milk
    - Zest of 1 lemon or 1 orange (optional, for extra flavor)
- **For the Syrup:**
    - 1 cup granulated sugar
    - 1 cup water
    - 1/4 cup lemon juice or orange juice
    - 1 teaspoon vanilla extract

Instructions:

1. **Prepare the Syrup:**
    - In a saucepan, combine the sugar, water, lemon juice (or orange juice), and vanilla extract.
    - Bring to a boil over medium heat, stirring occasionally until the sugar dissolves.
    - Reduce heat and let it simmer for about 10 minutes. Remove from heat and let it cool.
2. **Prepare the Cake Batter:**
    - Preheat your oven to 350°F (175°C).
    - Grease and flour a 9x13-inch baking dish or a similar-sized pan.
    - In a large bowl, beat the eggs and sugar together until light and fluffy.
    - Add the melted butter and yogurt, and mix well.
    - In a separate bowl, combine the semolina, flour, baking powder, and lemon or orange zest (if using).
    - Gradually add the dry ingredients to the wet ingredients, mixing until just combined.
    - Stir in the milk until the batter is smooth.
3. **Bake the Cake:**
    - Pour the batter into the prepared baking dish and smooth the top with a spatula.

- Bake in the preheated oven for about 30-35 minutes, or until the cake is golden brown and a toothpick inserted into the center comes out clean.
4. **Add the Syrup:**
    - Once the cake is done baking, remove it from the oven and immediately pour the cooled syrup evenly over the hot cake.
    - Allow the cake to absorb the syrup and cool completely before serving. This helps the syrup penetrate the cake and makes it moist and flavorful.
5. **Serve:**
    - Cut the revani into squares or diamonds and serve.

Tips:

- **Flavor Variations:** You can infuse the syrup with additional flavors, such as a cinnamon stick or a splash of orange blossom water.
- **Texture:** For a slightly denser texture, use full-fat yogurt or add a bit more semolina.

Enjoy this sweet, moist cake as a delicious finish to your meal or as a sweet treat throughout the day!

Halva

Ingredients:

- **For the Halva:**
    - 1 cup semolina
    - 1/2 cup unsalted butter or olive oil
    - 1 cup granulated sugar
    - 2 cups water
    - 1/2 cup raisins (optional)
    - 1/2 cup chopped nuts (optional, such as almonds or walnuts)
    - 1 teaspoon ground cinnamon
    - 1/2 teaspoon ground cloves (optional)
- **For the Syrup (Optional):**
    - 1 cup granulated sugar
    - 1 cup water
    - 1 teaspoon vanilla extract
    - 1/2 teaspoon lemon juice

Instructions:

1. **Prepare the Syrup (Optional):**
    - In a saucepan, combine the sugar, water, vanilla extract, and lemon juice.
    - Bring to a boil over medium heat, stirring until the sugar dissolves.
    - Reduce heat and simmer for about 10 minutes. Remove from heat and let it cool. This syrup can be drizzled over the halva when serving.
2. **Prepare the Halva:**
    - In a large skillet or saucepan, melt the butter or heat the olive oil over medium heat.
    - Add the semolina and cook, stirring frequently, until it turns a golden brown color. This can take 5-10 minutes.
    - In a separate saucepan, bring the water to a boil. Stir in the sugar until it dissolves.
    - Carefully pour the hot water and sugar mixture into the browned semolina, stirring continuously. Be cautious as the mixture may bubble and steam.
    - Stir in the raisins, nuts, cinnamon, and cloves (if using).
    - Reduce the heat to low, cover the pan, and simmer for about 10-15 minutes, or until the liquid is absorbed and the semolina is tender. Stir occasionally to prevent sticking.
3. **Set the Halva:**
    - Once cooked, remove the pan from heat and let the halva sit, covered, for about 10 minutes to firm up.

- Fluff the halva with a fork before serving.
4. **Serve:**
   - Halva can be served warm, at room temperature, or chilled. It can be drizzled with the optional syrup if desired.

Tips:

- **Texture:** For a creamier texture, you can substitute part of the water with milk.
- **Flavor Variations:** Feel free to add other spices like nutmeg or cardamom to suit your taste.
- **Nuts and Fruits:** Experiment with different nuts and dried fruits to customize the flavor and texture.

Enjoy your homemade halva as a delightful dessert or a sweet snack!

Kataifi

Ingredients:

- **For the Kataifi:**
    - 1 package (16 oz) kataifi dough (shredded phyllo dough), thawed
    - 1 cup unsalted butter, melted
    - 1 cup walnuts or pistachios, finely chopped
    - 1/2 cup granulated sugar
    - 1 teaspoon ground cinnamon
- **For the Syrup:**
    - 1 cup granulated sugar
    - 1 cup water
    - 1/2 cup honey
    - 1 teaspoon vanilla extract
    - 1 teaspoon lemon juice

Instructions:

1. **Prepare the Syrup:**
    - In a saucepan, combine the sugar, water, honey, vanilla extract, and lemon juice.
    - Bring to a boil over medium heat, stirring occasionally until the sugar dissolves.
    - Reduce heat and let it simmer for about 10 minutes. Remove from heat and let it cool to room temperature.
2. **Prepare the Filling:**
    - In a bowl, combine the chopped nuts, granulated sugar, and ground cinnamon.
3. **Assemble the Kataifi:**
    - Preheat your oven to 350°F (175°C).
    - Brush a 9x13-inch baking dish with melted butter.
    - Gently separate the kataifi dough with your fingers to loosen it. Spread about half of the kataifi dough evenly in the bottom of the prepared baking dish. Brush generously with melted butter.
    - Evenly spread the nut mixture over the kataifi dough.
    - Top with the remaining kataifi dough, spreading it out and brushing each layer generously with melted butter.
4. **Bake:**
    - Bake in the preheated oven for about 45-50 minutes, or until the kataifi is golden brown and crisp.
5. **Add the Syrup:**
    - Once the kataifi is done baking, remove it from the oven and immediately pour the cooled syrup evenly over the hot pastry.

- Allow the kataifi to cool completely in the pan before cutting into squares or diamond shapes.
6. **Serve:**
   - Enjoy your kataifi at room temperature or slightly warm.

Tips:

- **Butter Application:** Be generous with the butter to ensure that the kataifi dough becomes crispy and golden.
- **Nuts:** Feel free to mix different types of nuts or adjust the amount based on your preference.
- **Syrup:** If you like a more intense syrup flavor, you can add a little more honey or vanilla extract to the syrup mixture.

Kataifi is a wonderful dessert that combines the crunchiness of the dough with the sweetness of the syrup and the richness of the nuts. Enjoy this delicious treat with a cup of tea or coffee!

Karpatka

Ingredients:

- **For the Pastry:**
    - 1 cup (230 grams) unsalted butter
    - 1 cup (240 ml) water
    - 1 cup (120 grams) all-purpose flour
    - 4 large eggs
- **For the Custard Filling:**
    - 2 cups (480 ml) milk
    - 1 cup (200 grams) granulated sugar
    - 4 large egg yolks
    - 1/4 cup (30 grams) all-purpose flour
    - 2 tablespoons cornstarch
    - 1 teaspoon vanilla extract
    - 2 tablespoons unsalted butter
- **For Dusting (Optional):**
    - Powdered sugar

Instructions:

1. **Prepare the Pastry:**
    - Preheat your oven to 400°F (200°C).
    - In a medium saucepan, bring the butter and water to a boil over medium heat.
    - Once boiling, remove from heat and add the flour all at once. Stir vigorously until the mixture forms a smooth dough.
    - Return the pan to the heat and cook, stirring constantly, for about 1-2 minutes, until the dough starts to pull away from the sides of the pan.
    - Transfer the dough to a large bowl and let it cool for a few minutes.
    - Beat in the eggs one at a time, mixing well after each addition. The dough should be smooth and glossy.
    - Divide the dough in half. Spread each half evenly onto separate parchment-lined baking sheets, forming rectangles or squares.
    - Bake in the preheated oven for 20-25 minutes, or until the pastry is golden brown and puffed. Remove from the oven and let cool completely.
2. **Prepare the Custard Filling:**
    - In a medium saucepan, heat the milk over medium heat until it is hot but not boiling.
    - In a separate bowl, whisk together the sugar, egg yolks, flour, and cornstarch until smooth.
    - Gradually whisk a small amount of the hot milk into the egg mixture to temper it.

- Pour the tempered egg mixture back into the saucepan with the remaining milk.
- Cook the mixture over medium heat, whisking constantly, until it thickens and comes to a boil. This should take about 2-3 minutes.
- Remove from heat and stir in the vanilla extract and butter until smooth.
- Transfer the custard to a bowl, cover with plastic wrap (press the wrap directly onto the surface of the custard to prevent a skin from forming), and let it cool to room temperature.

3. **Assemble the Karpatka:**
    - Place one layer of the cooled pastry on a serving platter.
    - Spread the custard evenly over the first layer.
    - Top with the second layer of pastry, pressing down gently to ensure it sticks to the custard.

4. **Finish and Serve:**
    - Dust the top of the Karpatka with powdered sugar if desired.
    - Chill in the refrigerator for at least 2 hours to allow the filling to set before slicing and serving.

Tips:

- **Pastry Layers:** Make sure the pastry layers are completely cooled before adding the custard to prevent it from melting or becoming soggy.
- **Custard Texture:** If the custard seems too thick, you can whisk in a bit more milk to reach the desired consistency.

Karpatka is a delightful dessert that's sure to impress with its crispy pastry and rich custard filling. Enjoy!

Bougatsa

Ingredients:

- **For the Pastry:**
    - 1 package (16 oz) phyllo dough, thawed
    - 1/2 cup unsalted butter, melted (for brushing the phyllo)
- **For the Custard Filling:**
    - 2 cups milk
    - 1 cup granulated sugar
    - 1/2 cup semolina (fine or medium)
    - 3 large eggs
    - 1 teaspoon vanilla extract
    - 2 tablespoons unsalted butter
- **For Garnish (Optional):**
    - Powdered sugar
    - Ground cinnamon

Instructions:

1. **Prepare the Custard Filling:**
    - In a medium saucepan, heat the milk over medium heat until it is hot but not boiling.
    - In a separate bowl, whisk together the sugar and semolina.
    - Gradually whisk in a small amount of the hot milk to temper the mixture.
    - Pour the tempered mixture back into the saucepan with the remaining hot milk.
    - Cook over medium heat, stirring constantly, until the mixture thickens and comes to a boil. This should take about 5-7 minutes.
    - Remove from heat and stir in the vanilla extract and butter until smooth.
    - Transfer the custard to a bowl and cover it with plastic wrap, pressing the wrap directly onto the surface of the custard to prevent a skin from forming. Allow it to cool to room temperature.
2. **Prepare the Phyllo Pastry:**
    - Preheat your oven to 350°F (175°C).
    - Brush a 9x13-inch baking dish with melted butter.
    - Carefully lay one sheet of phyllo dough into the prepared dish and brush it with melted butter. Repeat with about 8-10 sheets, brushing each layer with butter.
    - Spread the cooled custard evenly over the layered phyllo.
3. **Add the Top Layers:**
    - Continue layering the remaining phyllo dough on top of the custard, brushing each layer with melted butter, until you have about 8-10 layers on top. Be sure to cover the custard completely.

- Brush the top layer with melted butter.
4. **Bake the Bougatsa:**
    - Bake in the preheated oven for about 40-45 minutes, or until the phyllo is golden brown and crisp.
5. **Finish and Serve:**
    - Allow the bougatsa to cool slightly before cutting into squares or rectangles.
    - Dust with powdered sugar and ground cinnamon just before serving, if desired.

Tips:

- **Phyllo Dough:** Be sure to keep the phyllo dough covered with a damp cloth while working to prevent it from drying out.
- **Custard Thickness:** If the custard seems too thick or too thin, adjust the amount of semolina or milk accordingly. It should be thick enough to spread but not too stiff.
- **Serving:** Bougatsa is best served warm or at room temperature.

Enjoy this delightful Greek pastry with a cup of coffee or tea!

Melomakarona

Ingredients:

- **For the Cookies:**
    - 1 cup (225 grams) unsalted butter, softened
    - 1 cup (200 grams) granulated sugar
    - 1/2 cup (120 ml) freshly squeezed orange juice
    - 1/4 cup (60 ml) brandy or water
    - 1/2 cup (60 grams) finely chopped walnuts (optional)
    - 1 teaspoon baking powder
    - 1 teaspoon ground cinnamon
    - 1/4 teaspoon ground cloves
    - 4 cups (500 grams) all-purpose flour
- **For the Syrup:**
    - 1 cup (240 ml) honey
    - 1 cup (200 grams) granulated sugar
    - 1 cup (240 ml) water
    - 1 cinnamon stick
    - 2-3 whole cloves
    - 1 teaspoon vanilla extract (optional)
- **For Garnish:**
    - 1/2 cup (60 grams) finely chopped walnuts
    - Ground cinnamon (optional)

Instructions:

1. **Prepare the Syrup:**
    - In a saucepan, combine the honey, sugar, and water.
    - Add the cinnamon stick and cloves.
    - Bring to a boil, then reduce the heat and simmer for about 10 minutes, until the syrup slightly thickens.
    - Remove from heat and stir in the vanilla extract if using. Let the syrup cool.
2. **Prepare the Cookies:**
    - Preheat your oven to 350°F (175°C). Line baking sheets with parchment paper.
    - In a large bowl, cream together the softened butter and sugar until light and fluffy.
    - Mix in the orange juice and brandy (or water).
    - In another bowl, combine the flour, baking powder, cinnamon, and cloves.
    - Gradually add the dry ingredients to the wet ingredients, mixing until just combined. The dough should be soft but manageable.
    - If using, fold in the finely chopped walnuts.
3. **Shape and Bake the Cookies:**

- Take small portions of dough (about 1 tablespoon each) and shape them into oval or round cookies.
- Place them on the prepared baking sheets.
- Use a fork to lightly press down on each cookie, creating a pattern.
- Bake in the preheated oven for about 20-25 minutes, or until the cookies are lightly golden.

4. **Soak the Cookies:**
   - While the cookies are still warm, dip them into the cooled syrup for a few seconds to soak them.
   - Remove the cookies from the syrup and place them on a wire rack to drain and cool.

5. **Garnish:**
   - While the cookies are still tacky from the syrup, sprinkle them with finely chopped walnuts and a dusting of ground cinnamon if desired.

Tips:

- **Texture:** Melomakarona should be soft and moist on the inside, with a slightly crisp edge. Don't overbake them.
- **Flavor:** You can adjust the spices to your taste. Adding a bit of grated orange zest to the dough can enhance the flavor.
- **Storage:** These cookies can be stored in an airtight container for up to a week. They often taste even better after a day or two as the flavors meld.

Melomakarona are a beloved treat during the holiday season and are sure to be a hit with family and friends. Enjoy these sweet, spiced cookies with a cup of tea or coffee!

Kourabiedes

Ingredients:

- **For the Cookies:**
    - 1 cup (225 grams) unsalted butter, softened
    - 1/2 cup (100 grams) granulated sugar
    - 1/2 cup (70 grams) chopped almonds (or other nuts like walnuts or pistachios)
    - 1 large egg yolk
    - 1 teaspoon vanilla extract
    - 1/4 cup (60 ml) brandy or milk (optional, for extra flavor)
    - 2 1/2 cups (300 grams) all-purpose flour
    - 1/4 teaspoon baking powder
    - Pinch of salt
- **For Dusting:**
    - 1 cup (120 grams) powdered sugar
    - Ground cinnamon (optional, for sprinkling)

Instructions:

1. **Prepare the Dough:**
    - Preheat your oven to 350°F (175°C). Line baking sheets with parchment paper.
    - In a large bowl, cream together the softened butter and granulated sugar until light and fluffy.
    - Mix in the egg yolk, vanilla extract, and brandy (if using).
    - In another bowl, combine the flour, baking powder, and salt.
    - Gradually add the dry ingredients to the wet ingredients, mixing until just combined.
    - Fold in the chopped almonds.
2. **Shape the Cookies:**
    - Take small portions of dough (about 1 tablespoon each) and roll them into balls. You can also shape them into crescents or other shapes if desired.
    - Place the shaped cookies on the prepared baking sheets, spacing them about 1 inch apart.
    - Gently press down on each cookie with the back of a fork or your fingers to flatten slightly.
3. **Bake the Cookies:**
    - Bake in the preheated oven for about 15-20 minutes, or until the cookies are lightly golden on the edges.
    - Be careful not to overbake them; they should remain pale in color.
4. **Dust with Powdered Sugar:**

- Allow the cookies to cool slightly on the baking sheets before transferring them to a wire rack to cool completely.
- Once cooled, generously dust the cookies with powdered sugar. If desired, you can also sprinkle a little ground cinnamon on top for extra flavor.

5. **Serve:**
    - Enjoy the kourabiedes with coffee or tea. They can be stored in an airtight container at room temperature for up to a week.

Tips:

- **Butter:** For the best texture, make sure your butter is softened but not melted.
- **Texture:** The dough should be soft and slightly crumbly. If it feels too dry, you can add a bit more milk or brandy to moisten it.
- **Nuts:** Toasting the nuts lightly before chopping them can enhance their flavor.

Kourabiedes are a delightful treat that captures the essence of Greek holiday baking. Their buttery, nutty flavor and snowy powdered sugar coating make them a festive favorite. Enjoy!

Sokolatopita

Ingredients:

- **For the Filling:**
    - 1 cup (240 ml) heavy cream
    - 1 cup (175 grams) semi-sweet or dark chocolate chips (or chopped chocolate)
    - 1/4 cup (60 ml) milk
    - 3 large eggs
    - 1/4 cup (50 grams) granulated sugar
    - 1 teaspoon vanilla extract
- **For the Crust:**
    - 1 package (16 oz) phyllo dough, thawed
    - 1/2 cup (115 grams) unsalted butter, melted
    - 1/4 cup (50 grams) granulated sugar (optional, for added sweetness)
- **For Garnish (Optional):**
    - Powdered sugar
    - Whipped cream
    - Fresh berries

Instructions:

1. **Prepare the Crust:**
    - Preheat your oven to 350°F (175°C). Grease a 9-inch (23 cm) pie dish or a similar-sized baking dish.
    - Lay one sheet of phyllo dough in the prepared dish and brush it with melted butter. Repeat this process, layering and brushing each sheet with butter, until you have 6-8 sheets layered.
    - If using, sprinkle a little granulated sugar between some layers for added sweetness.
    - Fold and trim the edges of the phyllo dough to fit the dish, creating a rustic look. Brush the top layer with melted butter.
    - Bake in the preheated oven for about 10 minutes, or until the phyllo is golden and crisp. Remove from the oven and let it cool slightly.
2. **Prepare the Filling:**
    - In a saucepan, heat the heavy cream and milk over medium heat until it starts to simmer. Do not let it boil.
    - Remove from heat and add the chocolate chips, stirring until the chocolate is completely melted and the mixture is smooth.
    - In a bowl, whisk together the eggs, granulated sugar, and vanilla extract.
    - Gradually whisk the warm chocolate mixture into the egg mixture, combining well.
3. **Assemble and Bake:**

- Pour the chocolate filling into the pre-baked phyllo crust.
- Return to the oven and bake for 25-30 minutes, or until the filling is set and the top is slightly puffed. The center should still be slightly soft but not liquid.

4. **Cool and Serve:**
   - Allow the Sokolatopita to cool to room temperature before slicing. It will set further as it cools.
   - Garnish with powdered sugar, whipped cream, and fresh berries if desired.

Tips:

- **Phyllo Dough:** Keep the phyllo dough covered with a damp cloth while working to prevent it from drying out.
- **Chocolate:** Use high-quality chocolate for the best flavor. Semi-sweet or dark chocolate works well.
- **Texture:** The filling should be creamy and slightly soft in the center. Avoid overbaking to ensure a smooth texture.

Sokolatopita is a decadent and satisfying dessert that brings together the crispy texture of phyllo and the rich, creamy chocolate filling. Perfect for special occasions or a treat anytime!

Chiboust

Ingredients:

- **For the Pastry Cream:**
    - 2 cups (480 ml) milk
    - 1/2 cup (100 grams) granulated sugar
    - 4 large egg yolks
    - 1/4 cup (30 grams) all-purpose flour
    - 1 tablespoon cornstarch
    - 1 teaspoon vanilla extract
    - 2 tablespoons unsalted butter
- **For the Meringue:**
    - 3 large egg whites
    - 1/2 cup (100 grams) granulated sugar
    - 1/4 teaspoon cream of tartar (optional, for stability)

Instructions:

1. **Prepare the Pastry Cream:**
    - In a medium saucepan, heat the milk over medium heat until it's hot but not boiling.
    - In a bowl, whisk together the sugar, egg yolks, flour, and cornstarch until smooth.
    - Gradually add a small amount of the hot milk to the egg mixture to temper it, whisking continuously.
    - Pour the tempered egg mixture back into the saucepan with the remaining hot milk.
    - Cook the mixture over medium heat, whisking constantly, until it thickens and starts to bubble. This should take about 5-7 minutes.
    - Remove from heat and stir in the vanilla extract and butter until smooth.
    - Transfer the pastry cream to a bowl, cover with plastic wrap (pressing the wrap directly onto the surface to prevent a skin from forming), and let it cool to room temperature.
2. **Prepare the Meringue:**
    - In a clean, dry mixing bowl, beat the egg whites with an electric mixer on medium speed until they begin to foam.
    - Add the cream of tartar (if using) and continue to beat until soft peaks form.
    - Gradually add the sugar, a tablespoon at a time, while continuing to beat until stiff, glossy peaks form.
3. **Combine the Pastry Cream and Meringue:**

- Gently fold the cooled pastry cream into the meringue. Be careful not to deflate the meringue; use a light hand and fold until the mixture is well combined and smooth.
4. **Use or Store:**
    - The Chiboust cream is now ready to use as a filling or topping for your desserts. It can be piped into éclairs, used to fill tarts, or served as a standalone dessert.
    - If not using immediately, you can refrigerate the Chiboust cream in an airtight container for up to 2 days. Gently re-whip before using if necessary.

Tips:

- **Texture:** Ensure that both the pastry cream and meringue are at room temperature before folding them together to achieve a smooth, airy texture.
- **Stability:** If you want the cream to hold its shape for longer periods, you can stabilize it with a small amount of gelatin. Dissolve 1 teaspoon of gelatin in 2 tablespoons of water, then add it to the pastry cream before folding in the meringue.

Chiboust cream is a versatile and elegant filling that adds a light, airy touch to a variety of pastries and desserts. Enjoy experimenting with it in your favorite recipes!

Ekmek Kataifi

Ingredients:

- **For the Kataifi Base:**
    - 1 package (16 oz) kataifi dough (shredded phyllo dough), thawed
    - 1/2 cup (115 grams) unsalted butter, melted
    - 1/2 cup (50 grams) chopped walnuts (optional)
- **For the Custard:**
    - 2 cups (480 ml) milk
    - 1 cup (200 grams) granulated sugar
    - 4 large egg yolks
    - 1/4 cup (30 grams) all-purpose flour
    - 2 tablespoons cornstarch
    - 1 teaspoon vanilla extract
    - 2 tablespoons unsalted butter
- **For the Syrup:**
    - 1 cup (240 ml) water
    - 1 cup (200 grams) granulated sugar
    - 1/2 cup (120 ml) honey
    - 1 teaspoon lemon juice
    - 1 cinnamon stick (optional)
- **For Garnish (Optional):**
    - Ground cinnamon
    - Chopped nuts (such as walnuts or pistachios)

Instructions:

1. **Prepare the Kataifi Base:**
    - Preheat your oven to 350°F (175°C).
    - In a large bowl, gently loosen the kataifi dough with your fingers to separate the strands.
    - Brush a 9x13-inch baking dish with melted butter.
    - Spread half of the kataifi dough evenly in the bottom of the prepared dish. If using, sprinkle the chopped walnuts over the dough.
    - Brush the top of the kataifi with melted butter.
    - Bake in the preheated oven for 20-25 minutes, or until golden brown and crisp. Remove from the oven and set aside to cool.
2. **Prepare the Custard:**
    - In a medium saucepan, heat the milk over medium heat until hot but not boiling.
    - In a bowl, whisk together the sugar, egg yolks, flour, and cornstarch until smooth.
    - Gradually whisk a small amount of the hot milk into the egg mixture to temper it.

- Pour the tempered egg mixture back into the saucepan with the remaining hot milk.
- Cook over medium heat, whisking constantly, until the mixture thickens and comes to a boil. This should take about 5-7 minutes.
- Remove from heat and stir in the vanilla extract and butter until smooth.
- Allow the custard to cool slightly before spreading it over the cooled kataifi base.

3. **Prepare the Syrup:**
    - In a saucepan, combine the water, sugar, honey, and lemon juice.
    - If using, add the cinnamon stick.
    - Bring to a boil over medium heat, stirring occasionally until the sugar dissolves.
    - Reduce heat and let the syrup simmer for about 10 minutes. Remove from heat and let it cool.

4. **Assemble the Dessert:**
    - Pour the cooled custard evenly over the kataifi base.
    - Drizzle the cooled syrup over the custard layer.

5. **Garnish and Serve:**
    - Optionally, sprinkle ground cinnamon and additional chopped nuts on top.
    - Allow the Ekmek Kataifi to set and chill in the refrigerator for at least 2 hours before serving.

Tips:

- **Texture:** Make sure the kataifi is crispy before adding the custard to prevent sogginess.
- **Custard:** Ensure the custard is smooth and thickened properly to achieve the best texture.
- **Syrup:** The syrup should be cooled before adding it to the dessert to avoid melting the custard.

Ekmek Kataifi is a deliciously indulgent dessert with a beautiful combination of textures and flavors. Enjoy this treat as a special dessert for family gatherings or festive occasions!

Samosa

Ingredients:

For the Pastry:

- 2 cups (250 grams) all-purpose flour
- 1/4 cup (60 ml) vegetable oil or melted ghee
- 1/2 teaspoon salt
- 1/2 teaspoon caraway seeds (optional)
- Water, as needed (approximately 1/2 cup)

For the Filling:

- 2 large potatoes, peeled and diced
- 1 cup (150 grams) frozen peas (or fresh peas)
- 1 tablespoon vegetable oil
- 1 teaspoon cumin seeds
- 1 teaspoon mustard seeds (optional)
- 1 teaspoon turmeric powder
- 1 teaspoon ground coriander
- 1 teaspoon garam masala
- 1 teaspoon cumin powder
- 1/2 teaspoon chili powder (adjust to taste)
- Salt, to taste
- 2 tablespoons chopped fresh cilantro (coriander leaves)
- 1 tablespoon lemon juice

For Frying:

- Vegetable oil

Instructions:

1. Prepare the Dough:

1. In a large bowl, combine the flour, salt, and caraway seeds (if using).
2. Add the vegetable oil or melted ghee and rub it into the flour until the mixture resembles coarse crumbs.
3. Gradually add water, a little at a time, and knead to form a smooth, firm dough. It should be slightly elastic but not sticky.
4. Cover the dough with a damp cloth and let it rest for at least 30 minutes.

2. Prepare the Filling:

1. Boil the diced potatoes in salted water until tender, about 10-15 minutes. Drain and mash the potatoes.
2. In a large skillet, heat the vegetable oil over medium heat.
3. Add the cumin seeds and mustard seeds (if using). When they start to sizzle, add the turmeric powder, ground coriander, garam masala, cumin powder, and chili powder.
4. Sauté the spices for a few seconds until fragrant, then add the frozen peas and cook for another 2-3 minutes.
5. Stir in the mashed potatoes and mix well. Cook for another 5 minutes, seasoning with salt to taste.
6. Remove from heat and stir in the chopped cilantro and lemon juice. Allow the filling to cool.

3. Assemble the Samosas:

1. Divide the dough into golf ball-sized portions. Roll each portion into a thin circle about 6 inches (15 cm) in diameter.
2. Cut the circle in half to form two semi-circles.
3. Take one semi-circle and fold it into a cone shape, sealing the edge with a little water.
4. Fill the cone with the prepared filling, packing it tightly.
5. Seal the open edge of the cone by pinching and folding it over to form a triangular shape.
6. Repeat with the remaining dough and filling.

4. Fry the Samosas:

1. Heat vegetable oil in a deep pan or skillet to 350°F (175°C).
2. Fry the samosas in batches, being careful not to overcrowd the pan. Fry until golden brown and crispy, about 4-5 minutes per batch.
3. Remove the samosas with a slotted spoon and drain on paper towels.

5. Serve:

- Serve the samosas hot with tamarind chutney, mint chutney, or yogurt sauce.

Tips:

- **Dough Consistency:** The dough should be firm but pliable. If it's too dry, add a bit more water; if too sticky, add a little more flour.
- **Filling Variations:** You can also add cooked meat, lentils, or other vegetables to the filling.
- **Freezing:** Samosas can be prepared in advance and frozen before frying. To fry, cook from frozen, adding a few extra minutes to the cooking time.

Enjoy your homemade samosas as a delicious and satisfying snack!

Yiaourti me Meli

Ingredients:

- **For the Dessert:**
    - 2 cups (500 grams) Greek yogurt (full-fat or strained)
    - 1/4 cup (60 ml) honey (preferably Greek honey)
    - 1/4 cup (30 grams) chopped nuts (such as walnuts, almonds, or pistachios) - optional
- **For Garnish (Optional):**
    - Fresh fruit (such as berries or figs)
    - Ground cinnamon

Instructions:

1. **Prepare the Yogurt:**
    - Scoop the Greek yogurt into serving bowls or glasses.
2. **Add Honey:**
    - Drizzle honey generously over the yogurt. Adjust the amount of honey to your taste preference.
3. **Add Nuts:**
    - Sprinkle chopped nuts over the honey, if using. This adds a nice crunch and additional flavor.
4. **Garnish and Serve:**
    - Optionally, garnish with fresh fruit or a sprinkle of ground cinnamon for added flavor.
    - Serve immediately for the best texture, or chill in the refrigerator until ready to serve.

Tips:

- **Yogurt:** Use high-quality Greek yogurt for a creamy texture and rich flavor. Full-fat yogurt will give a more luxurious mouthfeel.
- **Honey:** The quality of honey can significantly impact the flavor, so choose a good quality or local honey.
- **Nuts:** Toasting the nuts lightly before sprinkling them on top can enhance their flavor.

Yiaourti me Meli is a perfect, quick dessert or a light breakfast option. It combines the tanginess of Greek yogurt with the sweetness of honey, making it a satisfying treat that's both healthy and delicious. Enjoy!

Greek Almond Cake

Ingredients:

For the Cake:

- 2 cups (200 grams) ground almonds (blanched or slivered)
- 1 cup (200 grams) granulated sugar
- 4 large eggs
- 1/2 cup (120 ml) vegetable oil
- 1 teaspoon vanilla extract
- 1 teaspoon baking powder
- 1 teaspoon ground cinnamon
- 1/4 teaspoon ground cloves
- Pinch of salt

For the Syrup:

- 1 cup (240 ml) water
- 1 cup (200 grams) granulated sugar
- 1/4 cup (60 ml) honey
- 1 cinnamon stick
- 1 teaspoon lemon juice

For Garnish (Optional):

- Powdered sugar
- Ground cinnamon
- Sliced almonds

Instructions:

1. **Prepare the Syrup:**
   - In a saucepan, combine the water, sugar, honey, and cinnamon stick.
   - Bring to a boil, stirring until the sugar dissolves.
   - Reduce the heat and let it simmer for about 10 minutes until slightly thickened.
   - Stir in the lemon juice and remove from heat. Let it cool.
2. **Prepare the Cake Batter:**
   - Preheat your oven to 350°F (175°C). Grease and flour a 9-inch (23 cm) round cake pan or a similar-sized baking dish.
   - In a large bowl, whisk together the eggs, sugar, and oil until well combined and slightly frothy.
   - Add the vanilla extract.

- In another bowl, mix the ground almonds, baking powder, ground cinnamon, ground cloves, and salt.
- Gradually fold the almond mixture into the egg mixture until just combined. Be careful not to overmix.

3. **Bake the Cake:**
   - Pour the batter into the prepared cake pan.
   - Bake in the preheated oven for 30-35 minutes, or until a toothpick inserted into the center comes out clean.
   - Remove the cake from the oven and let it cool in the pan for about 10 minutes.

4. **Soak the Cake:**
   - While the cake is still warm, carefully pour the cooled syrup over it. The cake will absorb the syrup as it cools.
   - Let the cake cool completely in the pan, allowing it to fully absorb the syrup.

5. **Garnish and Serve:**
   - Once the cake is completely cool, you can garnish it with powdered sugar, ground cinnamon, and sliced almonds if desired.
   - Slice and serve the cake.

Tips:

- **Texture:** The cake should be moist and flavorful with a tender crumb. The syrup adds sweetness and moisture, so be generous with it.
- **Almonds:** Ensure the almonds are finely ground to achieve the right texture. You can use store-bought ground almonds or process whole almonds in a food processor.
- **Syrup:** The syrup can be made ahead of time and stored in the refrigerator. Just reheat slightly before using.

Greek Almond Cake is a delightful dessert with a rich almond flavor and a sweet syrupy finish. It's perfect for special occasions or as a sweet treat with coffee or tea. Enjoy!

Greek Rice Pudding

Ingredients:

- **For the Rice Pudding:**
    - 1/2 cup (100 grams) short-grain or Arborio rice
    - 1/4 cup (50 grams) granulated sugar
    - 4 cups (960 ml) whole milk
    - 1 cup (240 ml) water
    - 1/4 teaspoon salt
    - 1 teaspoon vanilla extract
    - 1 tablespoon unsalted butter (optional)
- **For Garnish (Optional):**
    - Ground cinnamon
    - Raisins or dried fruit (optional)

Instructions:

1. **Cook the Rice:**
    - In a medium saucepan, combine the rice and water. Bring to a boil over medium heat.
    - Reduce heat to low, cover, and simmer for about 10-15 minutes, or until the water is absorbed and the rice is tender.
2. **Prepare the Pudding Mixture:**
    - In another saucepan, heat the milk over medium heat until it's warm but not boiling.
    - Add the sugar and salt to the milk, stirring until the sugar is dissolved.
3. **Combine Rice and Milk:**
    - Once the rice is cooked and the water is absorbed, add the warm milk mixture to the rice.
    - Cook over medium-low heat, stirring frequently, until the mixture thickens and becomes creamy. This should take about 20-25 minutes.
    - If desired, stir in the butter for added richness and creaminess.
4. **Add Flavoring:**
    - Remove the saucepan from heat and stir in the vanilla extract.
5. **Cool and Serve:**
    - Transfer the rice pudding to serving bowls or cups.
    - Allow it to cool to room temperature, or refrigerate it for a chilled version.
    - Before serving, garnish with a sprinkle of ground cinnamon and, if desired, raisins or dried fruit.

Tips:

- **Texture:** If the pudding thickens too much as it cools, you can stir in a little more milk to reach your desired consistency.
- **Creaminess:** For a creamier texture, you can use half-and-half or a combination of milk and cream instead of just milk.
- **Flavor Variations:** You can add a pinch of nutmeg or a bit of lemon zest for additional flavor.

Rizogalo is a versatile and beloved Greek dessert that's both simple and satisfying. Whether served warm or cold, it's a comforting treat that's sure to please. Enjoy!

Tzatziki Ice Cream

Ingredients:

- **For the Ice Cream Base:**
    - 2 cups (480 ml) Greek yogurt (full-fat or strained)
    - 1 cup (240 ml) heavy cream
    - 1 cup (200 grams) granulated sugar
    - 1/2 cup (120 ml) milk
    - 1/2 cup (120 ml) water
    - 1/4 cup (60 ml) lemon juice
    - 2 tablespoons chopped fresh dill
    - 2 tablespoons chopped fresh mint
    - 1 medium cucumber, peeled, seeded, and finely grated
    - 1/2 teaspoon garlic powder (optional)
    - 1/2 teaspoon salt, or to taste

Instructions:

1. **Prepare the Cucumber:**
    - Place the grated cucumber in a fine mesh sieve or cheesecloth, sprinkle with a pinch of salt, and let it sit for about 10 minutes to drain excess moisture.
    - After draining, squeeze out any remaining liquid from the cucumber.
2. **Mix the Ice Cream Base:**
    - In a large bowl, combine the Greek yogurt, heavy cream, sugar, milk, and water. Whisk until the sugar is completely dissolved.
    - Stir in the lemon juice, chopped dill, chopped mint, and grated cucumber.
    - If using, add the garlic powder and salt. Mix well.
3. **Churn the Ice Cream:**
    - Pour the mixture into an ice cream maker and churn according to the manufacturer's instructions. This usually takes about 20-25 minutes, depending on your ice cream maker.
4. **Freeze the Ice Cream:**
    - Transfer the churned ice cream to an airtight container and freeze for at least 2 hours, or until firm.
5. **Serve:**
    - Scoop the tzatziki ice cream into bowls or cones.
    - Garnish with a sprinkle of fresh dill or mint if desired.

Tips:

- **Texture:** If you don't have an ice cream maker, you can pour the mixture into a shallow dish and freeze it. Stir every 30 minutes for the first 2-3 hours to break up ice crystals and ensure a creamy texture.
- **Flavor Balance:** Adjust the amount of garlic powder and salt to taste, depending on how pronounced you want the tzatziki flavors to be.
- **Garnish:** Fresh dill or mint makes a nice garnish that complements the flavors of the ice cream.

Tzatziki Ice Cream is a fun and unconventional dessert that combines savory and sweet elements. It's perfect for summer and can be a great conversation starter at gatherings. Enjoy this refreshing and unique treat!

Greek Donuts (Loukoumades)

Ingredients:

For the Dough:

- 1 cup (125 grams) all-purpose flour
- 1 tablespoon granulated sugar
- 1/2 teaspoon salt
- 1 tablespoon active dry yeast
- 3/4 cup (180 ml) warm water (about 110°F or 45°C)
- 1/4 teaspoon vanilla extract (optional)
- 1 tablespoon olive oil or vegetable oil

For Frying:

- Vegetable oil for deep frying

For the Syrup:

- 1 cup (240 ml) honey
- 1 cup (240 ml) water
- 1 cup (200 grams) granulated sugar
- 1 cinnamon stick (optional)

For Garnish:

- Ground cinnamon
- Chopped walnuts or almonds (optional)
- Sesame seeds (optional)

Instructions:

1. Prepare the Dough:

1. **Activate Yeast:**
    - In a small bowl, dissolve the yeast and a pinch of sugar in the warm water. Let it sit for about 5-10 minutes until frothy.
2. **Mix Dough:**
    - In a large mixing bowl, combine the flour, sugar, and salt.
    - Make a well in the center and pour in the yeast mixture, olive oil, and vanilla extract (if using).
    - Mix until a smooth, slightly sticky dough forms. The dough should be thick but not too dense.

3. **Let Dough Rise:**
   - Cover the bowl with a clean kitchen towel or plastic wrap.
   - Place it in a warm, draft-free area and let it rise for about 1 hour, or until doubled in size.

2. Prepare the Syrup:

1. **Cook Syrup:**
   - In a saucepan, combine the honey, water, sugar, and cinnamon stick (if using).
   - Bring to a boil, stirring occasionally until the sugar is fully dissolved.
   - Reduce heat and let it simmer for about 5 minutes, then remove from heat and allow it to cool slightly.

3. Fry the Loukoumades:

1. **Heat Oil:**
   - In a deep pot or large skillet, heat enough vegetable oil to submerge the donuts. Heat the oil to 350°F (175°C).
2. **Fry Donuts:**
   - Using two spoons or a small ice cream scoop, drop small spoonfuls of dough into the hot oil. Do not overcrowd the pot; fry in batches if necessary.
   - Fry the donuts for about 2-3 minutes per side, or until golden brown and crispy.
   - Remove with a slotted spoon and drain on paper towels.

4. Coat and Serve:

1. **Coat with Syrup:**
   - While the loukoumades are still warm, dip them into the warm syrup for a few seconds, then place them on a serving plate.
2. **Garnish:**
   - Sprinkle with ground cinnamon, chopped nuts, and/or sesame seeds if desired.
3. **Serve:**
   - Serve the loukoumades warm for the best flavor and texture.

Tips:

- **Oil Temperature:** Maintaining the correct oil temperature is crucial for getting crispy loukoumades. If the oil is too hot, they might burn on the outside while remaining uncooked inside. If too cool, they will absorb excess oil and become greasy.
- **Dough Consistency:** The dough should be sticky but manageable. If it's too runny, add a bit more flour; if too thick, add a bit more water.

Loukoumades are a delightful treat perfect for special occasions or as a sweet indulgence. Their combination of crispy exteriors and honey-soaked interiors makes them a favorite in Greek cuisine. Enjoy making and eating these delicious honey donuts!

Pita Me Meli

Ingredients:

For the Pie:

- 1 package (16 oz) phyllo dough, thawed
- 1 cup (225 grams) unsalted butter, melted (or use vegetable oil for a lighter version)
- 1 cup (200 grams) granulated sugar
- 1 cup (240 ml) honey (preferably Greek honey)
- 1 teaspoon vanilla extract
- 1/2 teaspoon ground cinnamon
- 1/4 teaspoon ground cloves (optional)
- 1/2 cup (50 grams) chopped walnuts or almonds (optional)

For Garnish (Optional):

- Powdered sugar
- Ground cinnamon

Instructions:

1. Prepare the Filling:

1. **Mix Filling:**
    - In a medium bowl, combine the granulated sugar, honey, vanilla extract, ground cinnamon, and ground cloves (if using). Mix well until the sugar is mostly dissolved.

2. Prepare the Phyllo Dough:

1. **Preheat Oven:**
    - Preheat your oven to 350°F (175°C). Grease a 9x13-inch baking dish or a similar-sized dish with a bit of melted butter.
2. **Layer Phyllo Dough:**
    - On a clean work surface, place one sheet of phyllo dough and brush it lightly with melted butter. Place another sheet of phyllo dough on top, brush with butter, and repeat until you have 8-10 layers. The more layers you use, the crispier the crust will be.
3. **Assemble the Pie:**
    - Spread a thin layer of the honey mixture over the phyllo dough, making sure to leave a border around the edges. If using, sprinkle a few chopped walnuts or almonds over the honey mixture.

- Continue layering the remaining phyllo dough on top, brushing each sheet with butter. You should have about 8-10 layers on top as well.
4. **Cut the Pie:**
   - Before baking, use a sharp knife to cut the pie into squares or diamond shapes. This will make it easier to serve after baking.

3. Bake the Pie:

1. **Bake:**
   - Bake in the preheated oven for 30-40 minutes, or until the phyllo is golden brown and crisp.
2. **Soak with Syrup:**
   - As soon as the pie comes out of the oven, pour the remaining honey mixture evenly over the hot pie. The syrup will soak into the layers of phyllo.
3. **Cool:**
   - Allow the pie to cool completely before serving. This will help the syrup absorb fully and the pie to set properly.

4. Garnish and Serve:

1. **Garnish (Optional):**
   - Before serving, you can dust the top with powdered sugar and additional ground cinnamon if desired.
2. **Serve:**
   - Cut along the pre-cut lines and serve the pie at room temperature.

Tips:

- **Phyllo Dough:** Make sure to keep the phyllo dough covered with a damp cloth while working to prevent it from drying out.
- **Butter:** Using melted butter gives a rich flavor, but you can substitute it with vegetable oil for a lighter version.
- **Serving:** Pita me Meli is often enjoyed as a dessert with tea or coffee.

This honey pie is a sweet and satisfying dessert with layers of crispy phyllo and a rich, honeyed filling. Enjoy this traditional Greek treat!

Kataifi Pie

Ingredients:

For the Custard Filling:

- 4 cups (960 ml) milk
- 1 cup (200 grams) granulated sugar
- 4 large egg yolks
- 1/4 cup (30 grams) all-purpose flour
- 2 tablespoons cornstarch
- 1 teaspoon vanilla extract
- 2 tablespoons unsalted butter

For the Kataifi Base:

- 1 package (16 oz) kataifi dough, thawed
- 1/2 cup (115 grams) unsalted butter, melted
- 1/2 cup (50 grams) chopped walnuts or almonds (optional)

For the Syrup:

- 1 cup (240 ml) water
- 1 cup (200 grams) granulated sugar
- 1/2 cup (120 ml) honey
- 1 teaspoon lemon juice
- 1 cinnamon stick (optional)

Instructions:

1. Prepare the Custard Filling:

1. **Heat Milk:**
   - In a medium saucepan, heat the milk over medium heat until it is hot but not boiling.
2. **Mix Egg Yolks:**
   - In a bowl, whisk together the sugar, egg yolks, flour, and cornstarch until smooth.
3. **Combine and Cook:**
   - Gradually whisk a small amount of the hot milk into the egg mixture to temper it.
   - Pour the tempered egg mixture back into the saucepan with the remaining hot milk.
   - Cook over medium heat, whisking constantly, until the mixture thickens and begins to boil. This should take about 5-7 minutes.

- Remove from heat and stir in the vanilla extract and butter until smooth. Set aside to cool slightly.

2. Prepare the Kataifi Base:

1. **Preheat Oven:**
   - Preheat your oven to 350°F (175°C).
2. **Prepare Kataifi Dough:**
   - In a large bowl, gently loosen the kataifi dough with your fingers to separate the strands.
3. **Butter Kataifi:**
   - Brush a 9x13-inch baking dish with melted butter.
   - Spread half of the kataifi dough evenly in the bottom of the prepared dish. If using, sprinkle the chopped walnuts or almonds over the dough.
   - Brush the top of the kataifi with more melted butter.
4. **Bake Kataifi:**
   - Bake in the preheated oven for about 20-25 minutes, or until golden brown and crispy. Remove from the oven and set aside.

3. Assemble the Pie:

1. **Add Custard:**
   - Pour the slightly cooled custard over the baked kataifi layer in the dish, spreading it evenly.
2. **Top with Remaining Kataifi:**
   - Spread the remaining kataifi dough over the custard layer, brushing it with more melted butter.
3. **Bake Again:**
   - Return the dish to the oven and bake for an additional 25-30 minutes, or until the top layer of kataifi is golden brown and crispy.

4. Prepare the Syrup:

1. **Cook Syrup:**
   - In a saucepan, combine the water, sugar, honey, and lemon juice.
   - If using, add the cinnamon stick.
   - Bring to a boil, stirring occasionally until the sugar dissolves.
   - Reduce heat and let the syrup simmer for about 10 minutes. Remove from heat and let it cool.

5. Serve:

1. **Soak with Syrup:**
   - While the pie is still warm, pour the cooled syrup evenly over the hot pie.
   - Allow the pie to cool completely before serving. This will help the syrup soak into the layers and set the custard.

2. **Garnish (Optional):**
   - Garnish with additional chopped nuts or a sprinkle of ground cinnamon if desired.

Tips:

- **Kataifi:** Ensure the kataifi dough is well separated and evenly layered for a crisp texture.
- **Custard:** Make sure to whisk constantly while cooking the custard to avoid lumps and ensure a smooth texture.
- **Syrup:** The syrup should be cooled before adding to the pie to prevent the custard from melting.

Kataifi Pie is a rich and flavorful dessert with a delightful combination of crispy, buttery layers and creamy custard. Enjoy this unique and indulgent Greek treat!

Rizogalo

Ingredients:

- **For the Rice Pudding:**
    - 1/2 cup (100 grams) short-grain or Arborio rice
    - 1/2 cup (100 grams) granulated sugar
    - 4 cups (960 ml) whole milk
    - 1 cup (240 ml) water
    - 1/4 teaspoon salt
    - 1 teaspoon vanilla extract
    - 1 tablespoon unsalted butter (optional)
- **For Garnish (Optional):**
    - Ground cinnamon
    - Raisins or dried fruit
    - Chopped nuts (such as almonds or walnuts)

Instructions:

1. Prepare the Rice:

1. **Cook Rice:**
    - In a medium saucepan, combine the rice and water. Bring to a boil over medium heat.
    - Reduce heat to low, cover, and simmer for about 10-15 minutes, or until the water is absorbed and the rice is tender.

2. Prepare the Pudding Mixture:

1. **Heat Milk:**
    - In another saucepan, heat the milk over medium heat until warm but not boiling.
    - Add the sugar and salt to the milk, stirring until the sugar is completely dissolved.
2. **Combine Rice and Milk:**
    - Once the rice is cooked and the water is absorbed, add the warm milk mixture to the rice.
    - Cook over medium-low heat, stirring frequently, until the mixture thickens and becomes creamy. This should take about 20-25 minutes.
3. **Add Flavor:**
    - Stir in the vanilla extract and butter (if using) until well combined.

3. Serve:

1. **Cool:**

- Transfer the rice pudding to serving bowls or cups. Allow it to cool to room temperature or refrigerate for a chilled version.
2. **Garnish:**
    - Before serving, garnish with a sprinkle of ground cinnamon and, if desired, raisins or dried fruit and chopped nuts.

Tips:

- **Texture:** If the pudding thickens too much while cooling, you can stir in a bit more milk to reach your desired consistency.
- **Flavor Variations:** You can add a pinch of nutmeg or a bit of lemon zest to the pudding for additional flavor.
- **Sweetness:** Adjust the sugar amount according to your taste preference.

Rizogalo is a versatile and comforting dessert that can be enjoyed warm or cold. Its creamy texture and subtle sweetness make it a beloved treat in Greek cuisine. Enjoy!

Greek Walnut Cake

Ingredients:

For the Cake:

- 1 1/2 cups (150 grams) finely ground walnuts
- 1 cup (200 grams) granulated sugar
- 4 large eggs
- 1/2 cup (120 ml) vegetable oil
- 1 teaspoon vanilla extract
- 1 cup (120 grams) all-purpose flour
- 1 teaspoon baking powder
- 1 teaspoon ground cinnamon
- 1/4 teaspoon ground cloves (optional)
- Pinch of salt

For the Syrup:

- 1 cup (240 ml) water
- 1 cup (200 grams) granulated sugar
- 1/4 cup (60 ml) honey
- 1 cinnamon stick (optional)
- 1 teaspoon lemon juice

For Garnish (Optional):

- Powdered sugar
- Ground cinnamon
- Chopped walnuts

Instructions:

1. Prepare the Syrup:

1. **Cook Syrup:**
   - In a saucepan, combine the water, sugar, honey, and cinnamon stick (if using).
   - Bring to a boil, stirring occasionally until the sugar is completely dissolved.
   - Reduce heat and let the syrup simmer for about 10 minutes.
   - Stir in the lemon juice, remove from heat, and let it cool.

2. Prepare the Cake:

1. **Preheat Oven:**

- Preheat your oven to 350°F (175°C). Grease and flour a 9-inch (23 cm) round cake pan or a similar-sized baking dish.
2. **Mix Wet Ingredients:**
    - In a large bowl, whisk together the eggs, sugar, vegetable oil, and vanilla extract until well combined.
3. **Mix Dry Ingredients:**
    - In another bowl, combine the ground walnuts, flour, baking powder, ground cinnamon, ground cloves (if using), and salt.
4. **Combine Mixtures:**
    - Gradually fold the dry ingredients into the wet ingredients until just combined. Be careful not to overmix.
5. **Bake Cake:**
    - Pour the batter into the prepared cake pan.
    - Bake in the preheated oven for 30-35 minutes, or until a toothpick inserted into the center comes out clean.
6. **Cool Cake:**
    - Allow the cake to cool in the pan for about 10 minutes, then transfer it to a wire rack to cool completely.

3. Soak the Cake:

1. **Pour Syrup:**
    - While the cake is still warm, pour the cooled syrup evenly over the cake. Allow the cake to absorb the syrup and cool completely.

4. Garnish and Serve:

1. **Garnish (Optional):**
    - Before serving, you can garnish the cake with powdered sugar, a sprinkle of ground cinnamon, and additional chopped walnuts if desired.
2. **Serve:**
    - Slice and serve the cake at room temperature.

Tips:

- **Texture:** The cake should be moist and flavorful. The syrup helps keep it tender and adds sweetness.
- **Walnuts:** Make sure to finely grind the walnuts to achieve the right texture and flavor.
- **Syrup:** Allow the syrup to cool before pouring it over the warm cake to prevent it from becoming too soggy.

Karydopita is a wonderful dessert with a rich walnut flavor and a sweet, spiced syrup. It's perfect for special occasions or as a comforting treat with coffee or tea. Enjoy this delightful Greek cake!

Melitzana Bougatsa

Ingredients:

For the Filling:

- 1 medium eggplant, peeled and diced
- 2 tablespoons olive oil
- 1 medium onion, finely chopped
- 2 cloves garlic, minced
- 1/2 cup (120 grams) feta cheese, crumbled
- 1/4 cup (60 grams) grated Parmesan cheese
- 1/4 cup (60 ml) milk or cream
- 2 large eggs
- 1/4 teaspoon dried oregano
- 1/4 teaspoon dried thyme
- Salt and freshly ground black pepper, to taste

For Assembling:

- 1 package (16 oz) phyllo dough, thawed
- 1/2 cup (115 grams) unsalted butter or olive oil, melted
- 1 tablespoon sesame seeds (optional)

Instructions:

1. Prepare the Filling:

1. **Cook the Eggplant:**
    - Heat the olive oil in a large skillet over medium heat.
    - Add the diced eggplant and cook, stirring occasionally, until it's tender and lightly browned. This should take about 8-10 minutes.
    - Remove the eggplant from the skillet and set it aside to cool slightly.
2. **Sauté Onions and Garlic:**
    - In the same skillet, add the chopped onion and cook until it's soft and translucent.
    - Add the minced garlic and cook for an additional 1-2 minutes.
3. **Combine Filling Ingredients:**
    - In a large bowl, combine the cooked eggplant, sautéed onion and garlic, crumbled feta cheese, grated Parmesan cheese, milk or cream, eggs, dried oregano, and dried thyme.
    - Season with salt and pepper to taste. Mix well until all the ingredients are combined.

2. Assemble the Bougatsa:

1. **Preheat Oven:**
    - Preheat your oven to 375°F (190°C). Grease a 9x13-inch baking dish or a similar-sized dish.
2. **Prepare Phyllo Dough:**
    - Lay one sheet of phyllo dough in the prepared baking dish and brush it lightly with melted butter or olive oil.
    - Repeat this process, layering and brushing each sheet, until you have about 6-8 layers.
3. **Add Filling:**
    - Spread the eggplant filling evenly over the layered phyllo dough.
4. **Top Layers:**
    - Continue layering phyllo dough on top of the filling, brushing each sheet with melted butter or olive oil. Use about 6-8 additional sheets to cover the filling.
5. **Finish and Bake:**
    - Brush the top layer with melted butter or olive oil and sprinkle with sesame seeds if desired.
    - Bake in the preheated oven for 30-35 minutes, or until the top is golden brown and crispy.

3. Serve:

1. **Cool and Cut:**
    - Allow the bougatsa to cool slightly before cutting into squares or slices.
2. **Enjoy:**
    - Serve warm or at room temperature. Melitzana Bougatsa is great as a snack, appetizer, or even a light meal.

Tips:

- **Phyllo Dough:** Keep the phyllo dough covered with a damp cloth while working to prevent it from drying out.
- **Eggplant:** Ensure the eggplant is well-cooked to avoid excess moisture in the filling, which could make the phyllo soggy.
- **Variations:** You can add other ingredients like sun-dried tomatoes, olives, or fresh herbs to the filling for extra flavor.

Melitzana Bougatsa combines the classic Greek pastry with the rich flavors of eggplant and cheese, creating a savory and satisfying dish that's perfect for a variety of occasions. Enjoy this delicious Greek treat!

Flogeres

Ingredients:

For the Pastry:

- 1 package (16 oz) phyllo dough, thawed
- 1/2 cup (115 grams) unsalted butter, melted (or use olive oil)
- 1/4 cup (60 ml) olive oil

For the Filling:

- 1 cup (200 grams) feta cheese, crumbled
- 1/2 cup (100 grams) grated Parmesan cheese
- 1/2 cup (100 grams) shredded mozzarella cheese (optional, for extra gooey texture)
- 1/4 cup (60 grams) ricotta cheese (optional, for creaminess)
- 1 large egg
- 1 tablespoon chopped fresh parsley (optional)
- 1 tablespoon chopped fresh dill (optional)
- Salt and freshly ground black pepper, to taste

Instructions:

1. Prepare the Filling:

1. **Combine Ingredients:**
   - In a medium bowl, mix together the crumbled feta, grated Parmesan, shredded mozzarella (if using), and ricotta (if using).
   - Add the egg, parsley, dill, salt, and pepper. Mix until well combined.

2. Prepare the Phyllo Dough:

1. **Preheat Oven:**
   - Preheat your oven to 375°F (190°C). Line a baking sheet with parchment paper.
2. **Assemble Phyllo Sheets:**
   - Lay one sheet of phyllo dough on a clean surface and brush it lightly with melted butter or olive oil.
   - Place another sheet on top and brush it with more butter or oil. Repeat this process until you have about 4-6 layers of phyllo dough.
3. **Cut Phyllo:**
   - Cut the stacked phyllo sheets into strips about 2 inches (5 cm) wide. You can also cut them into squares or rectangles if you prefer.

3. Assemble Flogeres:

1. **Add Filling:**
   - Place a small spoonful of the cheese filling at one end of each phyllo strip.
2. **Fold and Roll:**
   - Fold the sides of the phyllo strip over the filling to enclose it, then roll the strip into a log or spiral shape. You can also fold them into triangular shapes.
3. **Brush and Arrange:**
   - Brush the tops of the Flogeres with more melted butter or olive oil and place them on the prepared baking sheet.

4. Bake:

1. **Bake:**
   - Bake in the preheated oven for 15-20 minutes, or until the Flogeres are golden brown and crispy.
2. **Cool:**
   - Allow them to cool slightly on a wire rack before serving.

Tips:

- **Phyllo Dough:** Work with phyllo dough quickly to prevent it from drying out. Keep it covered with a damp cloth while you're working with it.
- **Filling Variations:** You can customize the filling with other cheeses, herbs, or even add ingredients like cooked spinach, mushrooms, or ham.
- **Shape:** If you prefer, you can make mini Flogeres by cutting the phyllo into smaller strips and making smaller rolls or spirals.

Flogeres are versatile and can be enjoyed as a snack, appetizer, or even a light meal. Their crispy exterior and flavorful filling make them a favorite in Greek cuisine. Enjoy your homemade Flogeres!

Kavourmas

Ingredients:

- 3 lbs (1.4 kg) pork belly or shoulder, cut into 1-inch (2.5 cm) cubes
- 1 cup (240 ml) olive oil
- 1 cup (240 ml) water
- 4 cloves garlic, minced
- 1 large onion, finely chopped
- 1 tablespoon dried oregano
- 1 tablespoon dried thyme
- 1 teaspoon ground cinnamon
- 1/2 teaspoon ground cloves
- 1/2 teaspoon ground black pepper
- 1 tablespoon paprika
- 1 bay leaf
- 1/4 cup (60 ml) red wine vinegar
- 1/2 cup (120 ml) white wine (optional, for extra flavor)
- Salt, to taste

Instructions:

1. Prepare the Pork:

1. **Season the Pork:**
   - In a large bowl, toss the pork cubes with salt, pepper, paprika, ground cinnamon, ground cloves, oregano, and thyme.

2. Cook the Pork:

1. **Sauté Aromatics:**
   - Heat a large pot or Dutch oven over medium heat and add 1/4 cup of olive oil.
   - Add the chopped onion and cook until it becomes translucent, about 5 minutes.
   - Add the minced garlic and cook for an additional 1-2 minutes until fragrant.
2. **Brown the Pork:**
   - Add the seasoned pork cubes to the pot and brown them on all sides. This should take about 5-7 minutes.
3. **Add Liquids:**
   - Once the pork is browned, add the remaining olive oil, water, red wine vinegar, and white wine (if using). Stir to combine.
4. **Simmer:**
   - Add the bay leaf and bring the mixture to a boil.
   - Reduce the heat to low, cover, and let it simmer gently for about 2-3 hours, or until the pork is tender and easily pulls apart. Stir occasionally.

3. Final Touches:

1. **Check Consistency:**
   - Once the pork is tender and cooked through, you may want to adjust the seasoning. If there's too much liquid, you can simmer it uncovered for a few more minutes to reduce it.
2. **Cool and Store:**
   - Remove the pot from heat and let the Kavourmas cool to room temperature.
3. **Refrigerate:**
   - Transfer the pork and its fat into an airtight container. Refrigerate. The Kavourmas can be stored in the refrigerator for up to a week. The fat will solidify and help preserve the meat.

Serving Suggestions:

- **Bread:** Serve Kavourmas with crusty bread or pita for a simple and satisfying meal.
- **Salads:** It pairs well with Greek salads or other fresh vegetable dishes.
- **Meze Platter:** It can be a great addition to a meze platter with olives, cheeses, and other small dishes.

Tips:

- **Fat Rendering:** The slow cooking process helps to render the pork fat, which keeps the meat tender and flavorful. If you prefer a leaner dish, you can use less fat.
- **Variations:** Some recipes include additional spices or herbs such as rosemary or bay leaf for different flavor profiles.

Kavourmas is a delicious and hearty dish that reflects the rich culinary traditions of Greece. Enjoy preparing and savoring this classic Greek recipe!

Bougatsa with Cream

Ingredients:

For the Cream Filling:

- 4 cups (960 ml) whole milk
- 1 cup (200 grams) granulated sugar
- 1/2 cup (100 grams) granulated sugar
- 4 large egg yolks
- 1/4 cup (30 grams) all-purpose flour
- 2 tablespoons cornstarch
- 1 teaspoon vanilla extract
- 2 tablespoons unsalted butter

For the Bougatsa:

- 1 package (16 oz) phyllo dough, thawed
- 1/2 cup (115 grams) unsalted butter, melted (or use vegetable oil)
- Powdered sugar (for dusting)
- Ground cinnamon (for dusting)

Instructions:

1. Prepare the Cream Filling:

1. **Heat Milk:**
    - In a medium saucepan, heat the milk over medium heat until it is hot but not boiling.
2. **Mix Egg Yolks:**
    - In a bowl, whisk together the egg yolks and sugar until smooth.
3. **Combine and Cook:**
    - Gradually whisk a small amount of the hot milk into the egg yolk mixture to temper it.
    - Pour the tempered egg yolk mixture back into the saucepan with the remaining hot milk.
    - Cook over medium heat, whisking constantly, until the mixture thickens and begins to bubble. This should take about 5-7 minutes.
    - Stir in the flour and cornstarch, and cook for an additional 2-3 minutes, until the mixture is thick and smooth.
    - Remove from heat and stir in the vanilla extract and butter until well combined.

- Transfer the cream filling to a bowl and let it cool to room temperature. Cover with plastic wrap, pressing it directly onto the surface of the cream to prevent a skin from forming.

2. Assemble the Bougatsa:

1. **Preheat Oven:**
   - Preheat your oven to 350°F (175°C). Grease a 9x13-inch baking dish or a similar-sized dish.
2. **Prepare Phyllo Dough:**
   - On a clean surface, lay one sheet of phyllo dough and brush it lightly with melted butter.
   - Place another sheet of phyllo dough on top, brush with butter, and repeat this process until you have about 6-8 layers.
3. **Add Cream Filling:**
   - Spread the cooled cream filling evenly over the phyllo dough.
4. **Top Layers:**
   - Continue layering the remaining phyllo dough on top of the cream filling, brushing each sheet with melted butter. Use about 6-8 additional sheets to cover the filling.
5. **Brush and Bake:**
   - Brush the top layer with melted butter.
   - Bake in the preheated oven for 30-35 minutes, or until the top is golden brown and crispy.

3. Serve:

1. **Cool:**
   - Allow the Bougatsa to cool slightly before cutting into squares or slices.
2. **Dust and Enjoy:**
   - Before serving, dust with powdered sugar and ground cinnamon if desired.

Tips:

- **Phyllo Dough:** Keep the phyllo dough covered with a damp cloth while working to prevent it from drying out.
- **Cream Filling:** Ensure the cream filling is completely cooled before spreading it onto the phyllo dough to prevent sogginess.
- **Texture:** The Bougatsa is best enjoyed warm or at room temperature, with a crispy top and creamy filling.

Bougatsa with Cream is a delightful Greek pastry with a crispy, buttery exterior and a rich, smooth custard filling. It's a wonderful treat for any occasion. Enjoy your homemade Bougatsa!

Amigdalopita

Ingredients:

For the Cake:

- 2 cups (200 grams) finely ground almonds (almond meal)
- 1 cup (200 grams) granulated sugar
- 1/2 cup (115 grams) unsalted butter, softened
- 4 large eggs
- 1 teaspoon vanilla extract
- Zest of 1 lemon
- 1 teaspoon baking powder
- Pinch of salt

For the Syrup (Optional):

- 1 cup (240 ml) water
- 1 cup (200 grams) granulated sugar
- 1/4 cup (60 ml) lemon juice
- 1 teaspoon vanilla extract

For Garnish (Optional):

- Powdered sugar
- Sliced almonds

Instructions:

1. Prepare the Syrup (If Using):

1. **Combine Ingredients:**
    - In a saucepan, combine the water, sugar, and lemon juice. Bring to a boil, stirring occasionally until the sugar is fully dissolved.
2. **Simmer:**
    - Reduce heat and let it simmer for about 10 minutes. Remove from heat and stir in the vanilla extract. Allow the syrup to cool.

2. Prepare the Cake:

1. **Preheat Oven:**
    - Preheat your oven to 350°F (175°C). Grease and flour an 8-inch (20 cm) round cake pan or a similar-sized baking dish.
2. **Mix Wet Ingredients:**

- In a large bowl, cream together the softened butter and sugar until light and fluffy.
- Beat in the eggs one at a time, mixing well after each addition.
- Stir in the vanilla extract and lemon zest.
3. **Combine Dry Ingredients:**
    - In another bowl, whisk together the ground almonds, baking powder, and a pinch of salt.
4. **Combine Mixtures:**
    - Gradually fold the dry ingredients into the wet mixture until well combined. The batter will be thick.
5. **Bake the Cake:**
    - Pour the batter into the prepared cake pan and smooth the top with a spatula.
    - Bake in the preheated oven for 35-40 minutes, or until a toothpick inserted into the center comes out clean.

3. Finish and Serve:

1. **Cool:**
    - Allow the cake to cool in the pan for about 10 minutes, then transfer it to a wire rack to cool completely.
2. **Apply Syrup (If Using):**
    - If you're using the syrup, pour the cooled syrup over the cake while it's still warm. Allow the cake to absorb the syrup and cool completely before serving.
3. **Garnish:**
    - Before serving, you can dust the cake with powdered sugar and garnish with sliced almonds if desired.

Tips:

- **Almonds:** Use finely ground almonds for the best texture. You can also pulse whole almonds in a food processor until finely ground.
- **Syrup:** The syrup adds extra moisture and sweetness to the cake. If you prefer a less sweet version, you can skip the syrup or use a smaller amount.
- **Storage:** Amigdalopita can be stored in an airtight container at room temperature for up to a week. The flavors often improve after a day or two.

Amigdalopita is a delightful almond cake that's both rich and fragrant. It's perfect for special occasions or as a comforting treat with coffee or tea. Enjoy your homemade Greek almond cake!

Greek Lemon Cake

Ingredients:

For the Cake:

- 1 1/2 cups (190 grams) all-purpose flour
- 1 1/2 teaspoons baking powder
- 1/4 teaspoon salt
- 1/2 cup (115 grams) unsalted butter, softened
- 1 cup (200 grams) granulated sugar
- 2 large eggs
- 1/2 cup (120 ml) milk
- 1/4 cup (60 ml) fresh lemon juice (about 1-2 lemons)
- Zest of 1 lemon
- 1 teaspoon vanilla extract

For the Lemon Glaze:

- 1 cup (120 grams) powdered sugar
- 2-3 tablespoons fresh lemon juice

Instructions:

1. Prepare the Cake:

1. **Preheat Oven:**
   - Preheat your oven to 350°F (175°C). Grease and flour an 8-inch (20 cm) round cake pan or a similar-sized baking dish. You can also line the pan with parchment paper for easier removal.
2. **Mix Dry Ingredients:**
   - In a medium bowl, whisk together the flour, baking powder, and salt. Set aside.
3. **Cream Butter and Sugar:**
   - In a large bowl, cream together the softened butter and granulated sugar until light and fluffy.
4. **Add Eggs and Flavors:**
   - Beat in the eggs one at a time, mixing well after each addition.
   - Stir in the lemon juice, lemon zest, and vanilla extract.
5. **Combine Mixtures:**
   - Gradually add the dry ingredients to the wet ingredients, alternating with the milk. Begin and end with the dry ingredients, mixing until just combined. Do not overmix.
6. **Pour and Bake:**

- Pour the batter into the prepared cake pan and smooth the top with a spatula.
- Bake in the preheated oven for 25-30 minutes, or until a toothpick inserted into the center comes out clean and the cake is golden brown.

7. **Cool:**
   - Allow the cake to cool in the pan for about 10 minutes before transferring it to a wire rack to cool completely.

2. Prepare the Lemon Glaze:

1. **Mix Glaze:**
   - In a small bowl, whisk together the powdered sugar and lemon juice until smooth. Adjust the consistency with more lemon juice or powdered sugar if needed.
2. **Glaze the Cake:**
   - Once the cake is completely cooled, drizzle the lemon glaze over the top. You can also spread it with a spatula for a more even layer.

Tips:

- **Lemon Juice:** Fresh lemon juice and zest give the best flavor. Avoid using bottled lemon juice if possible.
- **Texture:** For a lighter texture, you can sift the flour before measuring.
- **Storage:** The cake can be stored in an airtight container at room temperature for up to 3 days or in the refrigerator for up to a week. It also freezes well for up to 2 months.

Serving Suggestions:

- **With Tea or Coffee:** Greek Lemon Cake pairs beautifully with a cup of tea or coffee.
- **Toppings:** You can garnish the cake with additional lemon zest or thin lemon slices for a decorative touch.

This Greek Lemon Cake is perfect for any occasion, from casual gatherings to special celebrations. Its tangy lemon flavor and moist texture make it a delightful treat. Enjoy baking and savoring this refreshing cake!

Trahanopita

Ingredients:

For the Trahanas Mixture:

- 1 cup (150 grams) trahanas (fermented cracked wheat or bulgur; if unavailable, use fine bulgur or couscous)
- 1 1/2 cups (360 ml) water
- 1 cup (240 ml) milk (or more if needed)

For the Pie:

- 2 tablespoons olive oil
- 1 medium onion, finely chopped
- 2 cloves garlic, minced
- 1 cup (100 grams) crumbled feta cheese
- 1/2 cup (60 grams) grated Parmesan cheese
- 1/2 cup (60 grams) shredded mozzarella cheese (optional, for extra gooey texture)
- 2 large eggs
- 1/4 cup (60 ml) chopped fresh parsley
- 1 teaspoon dried oregano
- Salt and freshly ground black pepper, to taste
- 1 package (16 oz) phyllo dough, thawed (optional, for a crispy crust)

Instructions:

1. Prepare the Trahanas:

1. **Cook Trahanas:**
   - In a medium saucepan, bring the water and milk to a boil.
   - Add the trahanas and reduce the heat to low. Simmer, stirring occasionally, until the trahanas is cooked and has absorbed the liquid. This should take about 10-15 minutes.
   - Remove from heat and let it cool slightly.

2. Prepare the Pie Mixture:

1. **Sauté Aromatics:**
   - In a skillet, heat the olive oil over medium heat. Add the chopped onion and cook until softened, about 5 minutes.
   - Add the minced garlic and cook for an additional 1-2 minutes until fragrant.
2. **Combine Ingredients:**

- In a large bowl, mix together the cooked trahanas, sautéed onion and garlic, crumbled feta cheese, grated Parmesan cheese, shredded mozzarella cheese (if using), eggs, chopped parsley, and dried oregano.
- Season with salt and pepper to taste. Mix until well combined.

3. Assemble the Trahanopita:

1. **Preheat Oven:**
   - Preheat your oven to 375°F (190°C). Grease a 9-inch (23 cm) pie dish or a similar-sized baking dish.
2. **Using Phyllo Dough (Optional):**
   - If using phyllo dough, lay one sheet of phyllo in the prepared dish and brush it lightly with olive oil. Continue layering and brushing each sheet, about 6-8 layers, to create a base crust.
   - Pour the trahanas mixture into the prepared phyllo crust. Smooth the top with a spatula.
3. **Top Layers (if using phyllo):**
   - If you want a phyllo top, layer additional phyllo sheets over the filling, brushing each sheet with olive oil, as you did for the base. Use about 6-8 more sheets to cover the top.
4. **Bake:**
   - Bake in the preheated oven for 30-35 minutes, or until the top is golden brown and crispy, and the filling is set.

4. Serve:

1. **Cool:**
   - Allow the Trahanopita to cool slightly before slicing.
2. **Enjoy:**
   - Serve warm or at room temperature. It makes a great meal on its own or as part of a larger spread.

Tips:

- **Trahanas:** If you can't find trahanas, fine bulgur or couscous can be used as substitutes, though they won't have the same tangy flavor.
- **Phyllo Dough:** Using phyllo dough adds a crispy texture to the pie, but it's optional. The pie can also be baked without it for a more rustic presentation.
- **Cheese:** Feel free to experiment with different cheeses based on your preference.

Trahanopita is a comforting and flavorful dish with a unique taste from the trahanas. It's a wonderful example of Greek rustic cooking and is perfect for any meal of the day. Enjoy making and eating this hearty Greek pie!

Sweets of the Greek Gods

Ingredients:

For the Baklava:

- 1 package (16 oz) phyllo dough, thawed
- 1 cup (225 grams) unsalted butter, melted
- 2 cups (250 grams) finely chopped walnuts
- 1 cup (125 grams) finely chopped pistachios (optional)
- 1 cup (200 grams) granulated sugar
- 1 teaspoon ground cinnamon
- 1/2 teaspoon ground cloves

For the Syrup:

- 1 cup (240 ml) water
- 1 cup (200 grams) granulated sugar
- 1/2 cup (120 ml) honey
- 1 teaspoon vanilla extract
- 1 cinnamon stick
- 2-3 strips of lemon zest

Instructions:

1. Prepare the Filling:

1. **Mix Nuts and Spices:**
   - In a bowl, combine the chopped walnuts, pistachios (if using), granulated sugar, ground cinnamon, and ground cloves. Mix well and set aside.

2. Assemble the Baklava:

1. **Preheat Oven:**
   - Preheat your oven to 350°F (175°C). Grease a 9x13-inch (23x33 cm) baking dish with melted butter.
2. **Layer Phyllo Dough:**
   - Carefully unfold the phyllo dough and cover it with a damp cloth to prevent drying out.
   - Place one sheet of phyllo dough in the greased baking dish and brush it lightly with melted butter. Repeat this process, layering and buttering each sheet, until you have about 8-10 layers.
3. **Add Nut Filling:**
   - Sprinkle a thin, even layer of the nut mixture over the phyllo dough.
4. **Add More Phyllo Layers:**

- Continue layering phyllo sheets on top of the nut mixture, buttering each sheet as you go. Repeat until you have about 8-10 more layers on top.
5. **Cut and Bake:**
    - Using a sharp knife, cut the baklava into diamond or square shapes. Bake in the preheated oven for 45-50 minutes, or until the baklava is golden brown and crisp.

3. Prepare the Syrup:

1. **Cook Syrup Ingredients:**
    - While the baklava is baking, in a saucepan, combine the water, granulated sugar, honey, vanilla extract, cinnamon stick, and lemon zest. Bring to a boil, then reduce heat and let it simmer for about 10 minutes. Remove from heat and let it cool slightly.

4. Finish the Baklava:

1. **Pour Syrup:**
    - Once the baklava is done baking and still hot, remove it from the oven and pour the warm syrup evenly over the baklava. Make sure to cover all the pieces.
2. **Cool and Serve:**
    - Allow the baklava to cool completely before serving. The syrup will soak into the layers, making the baklava sweet and sticky.

Tips:

- **Phyllo Dough:** Keep the phyllo dough covered with a damp cloth while working to prevent it from drying out and becoming brittle.
- **Nuts:** Feel free to experiment with different nuts or nut combinations based on your preference.
- **Storage:** Baklava can be stored at room temperature in an airtight container for up to a week or in the refrigerator for longer storage.

Baklava is a decadent and aromatic dessert that brings together the richness of nuts and the sweetness of honey in a wonderfully crispy package. It's perfect for special occasions or as an indulgent treat any time of the year. Enjoy making and savoring this divine Greek dessert!

Vasilopita

Ingredients:

For the Cake:

- 1 cup (225 grams) unsalted butter, softened
- 1 cup (200 grams) granulated sugar
- 4 large eggs
- 1 cup (240 ml) milk
- 2 1/2 cups (300 grams) all-purpose flour
- 1 tablespoon baking powder
- 1/2 teaspoon salt
- 1 teaspoon vanilla extract
- Zest of 1 orange
- 1/4 cup (60 ml) freshly squeezed orange juice

For the Glaze:

- 1 cup (120 grams) powdered sugar
- 2-3 tablespoons milk
- 1/2 teaspoon vanilla extract

For Decoration:

- Whole almonds or chopped nuts (optional)
- A coin (wrapped in foil for safety)

Instructions:

1. Prepare the Cake Batter:

1. **Preheat Oven:**
   - Preheat your oven to 350°F (175°C). Grease and flour a 9-inch (23 cm) round cake pan or a similar-sized baking dish. You can also line the pan with parchment paper for easier removal.
2. **Cream Butter and Sugar:**
   - In a large bowl, cream together the softened butter and granulated sugar until light and fluffy.
3. **Add Eggs:**
   - Beat in the eggs one at a time, mixing well after each addition.
4. **Mix Dry Ingredients:**
   - In another bowl, whisk together the flour, baking powder, and salt.
5. **Combine Ingredients:**
   - Gradually add the dry ingredients to the butter mixture, alternating with the milk. Begin and end with the dry ingredients. Mix until just combined.
6. **Add Flavorings:**
   - Stir in the vanilla extract, orange zest, and orange juice.

7. **Add the Coin:**
   - If using a coin, wrap it in a small piece of foil and gently fold it into the batter, making sure it's well-distributed.

2. Bake the Cake:

1. **Pour Batter:**
   - Pour the batter into the prepared cake pan and smooth the top with a spatula.
2. **Bake:**
   - Bake in the preheated oven for 30-35 minutes, or until a toothpick inserted into the center comes out clean and the cake is golden brown.
3. **Cool:**
   - Allow the cake to cool in the pan for about 10 minutes before transferring it to a wire rack to cool completely.

3. Prepare the Glaze:

1. **Mix Glaze Ingredients:**
   - In a small bowl, whisk together the powdered sugar, milk, and vanilla extract until smooth. Add more milk if needed to reach the desired consistency.
2. **Glaze the Cake:**
   - Once the cake is completely cooled, drizzle the glaze over the top. You can also spread it with a spatula for a more even layer.

4. Decorate and Serve:

1. **Add Decoration:**
   - Decorate the cake with whole almonds or chopped nuts if desired.
2. **Cut and Serve:**
   - Serve the cake and enjoy the tradition of finding the hidden coin. Remember to inform your guests about the coin's presence.

Tips:

- **Coin Safety:** Ensure the coin is well-wrapped in foil to avoid any risk of contamination.
- **Flavor Variations:** You can add other flavorings like lemon zest or a splash of brandy to the batter for a different twist.
- **Storage:** The cake can be stored in an airtight container at room temperature for up to a week.

Vasilopita is not just a cake but a symbol of blessings and prosperity for the year ahead. It's a wonderful way to celebrate the New Year and honor Saint Basil's memory. Enjoy baking and sharing this special cake with family and friends!

Tiramisu Greek Style

Ingredients:

For the Cream Mixture:

- 1 cup (240 ml) heavy cream
- 1 cup (240 ml) Greek yogurt (full-fat or whole milk for best results)
- 1/2 cup (120 grams) granulated sugar
- 1 teaspoon vanilla extract
- 3 large egg yolks
- 1/4 cup (60 ml) honey
- 1/4 cup (60 ml) brewed coffee, cooled (strong espresso or regular coffee)

For the Layering:

- 1 package (7 oz, 200 grams) ladyfingers (savoiardi)
- 1/4 cup (60 ml) brewed coffee, cooled
- 1 tablespoon brandy or coffee liqueur (optional)

For Garnish:

- Unsweetened cocoa powder
- Ground cinnamon (optional)
- Chopped nuts (such as pistachios or almonds, optional)
- Fresh mint leaves (optional)

Instructions:

1. Prepare the Cream Mixture:

1. **Whip the Cream:**
   - In a large mixing bowl, whip the heavy cream until stiff peaks form. Set aside.
2. **Mix Egg Yolks and Sugar:**
   - In another bowl, whisk together the egg yolks and granulated sugar until pale and slightly thickened.
3. **Combine with Yogurt:**
   - Add the Greek yogurt and vanilla extract to the egg yolk mixture. Mix until smooth.
4. **Incorporate Honey:**
   - Stir in the honey until fully combined.
5. **Fold in Whipped Cream:**
   - Gently fold the whipped cream into the yogurt mixture until fully incorporated, taking care not to deflate the cream.

2. Prepare the Ladyfingers:

1. **Combine Coffee and Liqueur:**
   - In a shallow dish, combine the brewed coffee and brandy or coffee liqueur if using.
2. **Dip Ladyfingers:**
   - Briefly dip each ladyfinger into the coffee mixture, making sure not to soak them. Arrange them in a single layer at the bottom of your serving dish.

3. Assemble the Tiramisu:

1. **Layer Cream Mixture:**
   - Spread half of the cream mixture over the layer of dipped ladyfingers in the serving dish.
2. **Add Another Layer:**
   - Place another layer of dipped ladyfingers on top of the cream mixture.
3. **Top with Remaining Cream:**
   - Spread the remaining cream mixture evenly over the second layer of ladyfingers.

4. Chill and Serve:

1. **Chill:**
   - Cover the dish with plastic wrap and refrigerate for at least 4 hours, or overnight, to allow the flavors to meld and the dessert to set.
2. **Garnish:**
   - Before serving, dust the top with unsweetened cocoa powder and ground cinnamon if desired. Garnish with chopped nuts and fresh mint leaves for added flair.
3. **Serve:**
   - Cut into squares and serve chilled.

Tips:

- **Cream Consistency:** Ensure the cream is whipped well to give a light and airy texture to the dessert.
- **Flavor Adjustment:** Adjust the amount of honey or coffee to suit your taste preferences.
- **Make Ahead:** Tiramisu Greek Style can be made a day in advance, which helps the flavors develop and the texture set nicely.

This Greek-inspired tiramisu offers a fresh twist on the classic Italian dessert, blending the creamy richness of tiramisu with the tangy and sweet notes of Greek yogurt and honey. Enjoy this indulgent treat with a touch of Greek charm!

Greek Pumpkin Cake

Ingredients:

For the Cake:

- 1 1/2 cups (190 grams) all-purpose flour
- 1 teaspoon baking powder
- 1 teaspoon baking soda
- 1/2 teaspoon salt
- 1 teaspoon ground cinnamon
- 1/2 teaspoon ground nutmeg
- 1/4 teaspoon ground cloves
- 1/2 cup (115 grams) unsalted butter, softened
- 1 cup (200 grams) granulated sugar
- 2 large eggs
- 1 cup (240 ml) canned pumpkin puree (not pumpkin pie filling)
- 1/2 cup (120 ml) Greek yogurt or sour cream
- 1 teaspoon vanilla extract
- 1/2 cup (60 grams) chopped walnuts or pecans (optional)

For the Glaze (optional):

- 1 cup (120 grams) powdered sugar
- 2-3 tablespoons milk
- 1/2 teaspoon vanilla extract

Instructions:

1. Prepare the Cake Batter:

1. **Preheat Oven:**
   - Preheat your oven to 350°F (175°C). Grease and flour a 9-inch (23 cm) round cake pan or a similar-sized baking dish. You can also line the pan with parchment paper for easier removal.
2. **Mix Dry Ingredients:**
   - In a medium bowl, whisk together the flour, baking powder, baking soda, salt, cinnamon, nutmeg, and cloves. Set aside.
3. **Cream Butter and Sugar:**
   - In a large bowl, cream together the softened butter and granulated sugar until light and fluffy.
4. **Add Eggs:**
   - Beat in the eggs one at a time, mixing well after each addition.
5. **Add Pumpkin and Yogurt:**

- Stir in the pumpkin puree, Greek yogurt (or sour cream), and vanilla extract.
6. **Combine Mixtures:**
   - Gradually add the dry ingredients to the wet ingredients, mixing until just combined. If using, fold in the chopped walnuts or pecans.

2. Bake the Cake:

1. **Pour Batter:**
   - Pour the batter into the prepared cake pan and smooth the top with a spatula.
2. **Bake:**
   - Bake in the preheated oven for 30-35 minutes, or until a toothpick inserted into the center comes out clean and the cake is golden brown.
3. **Cool:**
   - Allow the cake to cool in the pan for about 10 minutes before transferring it to a wire rack to cool completely.

3. Prepare the Glaze (Optional):

1. **Mix Glaze Ingredients:**
   - In a small bowl, whisk together the powdered sugar, milk, and vanilla extract until smooth. Adjust the consistency with more milk or powdered sugar if needed.
2. **Glaze the Cake:**
   - Once the cake is completely cooled, drizzle the glaze over the top. You can also spread it with a spatula for a more even layer.

4. Serve:

1. **Cut and Enjoy:**
   - Slice the cake and serve. It can be enjoyed plain or with a dollop of whipped cream.

Tips:

- **Pumpkin Purée:** Use pure pumpkin purée, not pumpkin pie filling, for the best results.
- **Texture:** For a lighter cake, you can sift the flour before measuring.
- **Nuts:** The nuts are optional but add a nice texture and flavor.

This Greek Pumpkin Cake blends the warm spices of fall with the creamy richness of pumpkin and Greek yogurt, making it a deliciously comforting dessert. Perfect for gatherings or a cozy treat at home!

Mastiha Ice Cream

Ingredients:

- 1 cup (240 ml) milk
- 1 cup (240 ml) heavy cream
- 3/4 cup (150 grams) granulated sugar
- 4 large egg yolks
- 1-2 tablespoons mastiha powder (or crushed mastiha resin)
- 1 teaspoon vanilla extract
- A pinch of salt

Instructions:

1. Prepare the Mastiha Mixture:

1. **Crush Mastiha:**
   - If using mastiha resin, crush it into a fine powder using a mortar and pestle. If using mastiha powder, you can skip this step.

2. Make the Custard Base:

1. **Heat Milk and Cream:**
   - In a medium saucepan, combine the milk, heavy cream, and granulated sugar. Heat over medium heat until the mixture is hot but not boiling, stirring occasionally to dissolve the sugar.
2. **Whisk Egg Yolks:**
   - In a separate bowl, whisk the egg yolks until they are well combined.
3. **Temper the Egg Yolks:**
   - Gradually add a small amount of the hot milk mixture to the egg yolks, whisking constantly to temper them. This prevents the eggs from curdling.
4. **Combine Mixtures:**
   - Pour the tempered egg yolk mixture back into the saucepan with the remaining milk mixture. Cook over medium heat, stirring constantly, until the mixture thickens slightly and coats the back of a spoon. This should take about 5-7 minutes.
5. **Add Mastiha:**
   - Remove the saucepan from heat and stir in the crushed mastiha or mastiha powder, vanilla extract, and a pinch of salt.

3. Chill the Mixture:

1. **Cool Down:**

- Pour the custard mixture through a fine-mesh sieve into a clean bowl to remove any lumps or curdled bits. Allow it to cool to room temperature.
2. **Refrigerate:**
   - Cover the bowl with plastic wrap and refrigerate the mixture for at least 4 hours, or overnight, to chill completely.

4. Churn the Ice Cream:

1. **Prepare Ice Cream Maker:**
   - Follow the manufacturer's instructions for your ice cream maker. Make sure the bowl is properly chilled if required.
2. **Churn:**
   - Pour the chilled custard mixture into the ice cream maker and churn according to the manufacturer's instructions until it reaches a soft-serve consistency.

5. Freeze and Serve:

1. **Freeze:**
   - Transfer the churned ice cream to an airtight container and freeze for at least 2 hours to firm up.
2. **Serve:**
   - Scoop the ice cream into bowls or cones and enjoy the unique flavor of mastiha.

Tips:

- **Mastiha:** Mastiha can be found in specialty stores or online. If you can't find it, you might use a small amount of mastic extract as a substitute, but the flavor may not be as authentic.
- **Texture:** For a smoother texture, make sure to chill the custard thoroughly before churning.
- **Serving:** Allow the ice cream to sit at room temperature for a few minutes before serving to make scooping easier.

Mastiha Ice Cream is a delightful way to experience the distinctive flavor of mastiha, offering a unique twist on traditional ice cream flavors. Enjoy this refreshing and aromatic treat!

Greek Apricot Preserves

Ingredients:

- 2 pounds (900 grams) fresh apricots
- 2 cups (400 grams) granulated sugar
- 1/4 cup (60 ml) freshly squeezed lemon juice
- 1/2 cup (120 ml) water
- 1/2 teaspoon ground cinnamon (optional)
- 1/4 teaspoon ground cloves (optional)
- 1/4 cup (60 ml) honey (optional, for added richness)

Instructions:

1. Prepare the Apricots:

1. **Wash and Pit:**
   - Wash the apricots thoroughly. Cut them in half and remove the pits. You can leave the apricots in halves or cut them into smaller chunks, depending on your preference.

2. Cook the Preserves:

1. **Combine Ingredients:**
   - In a large, heavy-bottomed saucepan, combine the apricots, granulated sugar, lemon juice, and water. If using, add the ground cinnamon, ground cloves, and honey.
2. **Heat:**
   - Bring the mixture to a boil over medium-high heat, stirring frequently to dissolve the sugar.
3. **Simmer:**
   - Reduce the heat and let the mixture simmer gently. Continue to cook, stirring occasionally, for about 30-45 minutes, or until the apricots are tender and the mixture has thickened to a jam-like consistency.
4. **Check Consistency:**
   - To check if the preserves are ready, place a small amount of the mixture on a cold plate. Let it sit for a minute, then run your finger through it. If the line holds and the preserves are thick, they are done. If not, continue to cook for a few more minutes.

3. Sterilize Jars:

1. **Prepare Jars:**

- While the preserves are cooking, sterilize your canning jars and lids. Place them in a boiling water bath for 10 minutes or run them through a hot cycle in the dishwasher.

4. Jar the Preserves:

1. **Fill Jars:**
   - Carefully ladle the hot apricot preserves into the prepared sterilized jars, leaving about 1/4 inch (6 mm) of headspace at the top.
2. **Seal:**
   - Wipe the rims of the jars with a clean, damp cloth to remove any residue. Place the lids on top and screw on the bands until they are fingertip-tight.

5. Process and Store:

1. **Process (Optional):**
   - For longer storage, process the jars in a boiling water bath for 5-10 minutes. This step ensures a good seal and helps prevent spoilage.
2. **Cool:**
   - Allow the jars to cool completely at room temperature. You should hear a popping sound as the jars seal.
3. **Store:**
   - Store the sealed jars in a cool, dark place. The apricot preserves will keep for up to a year. Once opened, store in the refrigerator and use within a few weeks.

Tips:

- **Apricots:** Choose ripe, but firm apricots for the best flavor and texture.
- **Consistency:** If the preserves become too thick, you can stir in a little water to reach your desired consistency.
- **Flavor Variations:** Feel free to experiment with other spices or add a splash of vanilla extract for a different flavor profile.

Greek Apricot Preserves are a sweet and tangy treat that captures the essence of summer apricots. Enjoy them spread on toast, mixed into yogurt, or as a topping for desserts!

Almond Halva

Ingredients:

For the Halva:

- 1 cup (200 grams) semolina
- 1/2 cup (115 grams) unsalted butter or ghee
- 1/2 cup (75 grams) slivered almonds or chopped almonds
- 1 cup (200 grams) granulated sugar
- 2 cups (480 ml) water
- 1 teaspoon vanilla extract
- 1/4 teaspoon ground cinnamon (optional)

For Garnish (optional):

- Additional slivered or chopped almonds
- Ground cinnamon
- A sprinkle of powdered sugar

Instructions:

1. Prepare the Syrup:

1. **Combine Syrup Ingredients:**
   - In a medium saucepan, combine the granulated sugar and water. Heat over medium heat, stirring occasionally, until the sugar is completely dissolved. Bring to a simmer.
2. **Add Flavorings:**
   - Once the syrup is simmering, stir in the vanilla extract and ground cinnamon if using. Remove from heat and set aside.

2. Cook the Halva:

1. **Heat Butter and Nuts:**
   - In a large, heavy-bottomed skillet or saucepan, melt the butter or ghee over medium heat. Add the slivered or chopped almonds and cook, stirring frequently, until the almonds are golden brown and fragrant.
2. **Add Semolina:**
   - Add the semolina to the skillet with the butter and almonds. Cook, stirring constantly, for about 5-7 minutes or until the semolina is lightly toasted and golden brown.
3. **Combine with Syrup:**
   - Carefully pour the prepared syrup into the skillet with the semolina mixture. Be cautious as the mixture may bubble up.

4. **Cook Until Thickened:**
    - Stir continuously until the mixture thickens and starts to pull away from the sides of the pan. This should take about 10-15 minutes. The halva is done when it has a pudding-like consistency and has absorbed most of the syrup.

3. Set and Serve:

1. **Transfer to a Dish:**
    - Spoon the hot halva into a greased dish or mold, smoothing the top with a spatula. Let it cool at room temperature.
2. **Garnish:**
    - If desired, garnish the top with additional slivered almonds, a sprinkle of ground cinnamon, or a dusting of powdered sugar.
3. **Serve:**
    - Once cooled and set, cut the halva into squares or slices. Serve at room temperature or slightly warmed.

Tips:

- **Semolina:** Make sure to stir the semolina constantly while toasting to prevent it from burning.
- **Texture:** The halva will firm up as it cools. If it seems too runny when you first remove it from the heat, continue cooking it for a few more minutes until it thickens.
- **Flavor Variations:** You can experiment with other nuts or add a touch of cardamom for a different flavor profile.

Almond Halva is a delightful treat with a wonderful nutty flavor and a sweet, aromatic finish. It's a perfect way to enjoy a traditional Greek dessert with a comforting and rich taste. Enjoy!

Karpouzopita

Ingredients:

For the Cake:

- 4 cups (1 liter) watermelon, diced and seeds removed
- 1 cup (200 grams) granulated sugar
- 1/2 cup (120 ml) vegetable oil
- 2 large eggs
- 2 cups (240 grams) all-purpose flour
- 2 teaspoons baking powder
- 1/2 teaspoon baking soda
- 1/4 teaspoon salt
- 1 teaspoon vanilla extract
- 1/2 cup (120 ml) milk
- 1 tablespoon lemon juice

For the Syrup (optional):

- 1/2 cup (100 grams) granulated sugar
- 1/4 cup (60 ml) water
- 1 tablespoon lemon juice

For Garnish (optional):

- Powdered sugar
- Fresh mint leaves

Instructions:

1. Prepare the Watermelon:

1. **Remove Excess Liquid:**
    - Dice the watermelon and remove any seeds. Place the diced watermelon in a colander over a bowl to drain excess liquid. You want to remove as much moisture as possible to avoid a soggy cake.
2. **Mash Watermelon:**
    - Once drained, mash the watermelon with a fork or use a blender to puree it lightly, but leave some small chunks for texture.

2. Make the Cake Batter:

1. **Preheat Oven:**

- Preheat your oven to 350°F (175°C). Grease and flour a 9-inch (23 cm) round cake pan or a similar-sized baking dish. You can also line it with parchment paper for easier removal.
2. **Mix Wet Ingredients:**
   - In a large bowl, whisk together the granulated sugar, vegetable oil, and eggs until well combined.
3. **Add Watermelon:**
   - Stir in the mashed or pureed watermelon, mixing until evenly incorporated.
4. **Combine Dry Ingredients:**
   - In another bowl, whisk together the flour, baking powder, baking soda, and salt.
5. **Mix Together:**
   - Gradually add the dry ingredients to the wet ingredients, alternating with the milk. Begin and end with the dry ingredients. Mix until just combined. Stir in the vanilla extract and lemon juice.

3. Bake the Cake:

1. **Pour Batter:**
   - Pour the batter into the prepared cake pan and smooth the top with a spatula.
2. **Bake:**
   - Bake in the preheated oven for 35-45 minutes, or until a toothpick inserted into the center comes out clean and the cake is golden brown.
3. **Cool:**
   - Allow the cake to cool in the pan for about 10 minutes before transferring it to a wire rack to cool completely.

4. Prepare the Syrup (Optional):

1. **Combine Syrup Ingredients:**
   - In a small saucepan, combine the granulated sugar, water, and lemon juice. Heat over medium heat, stirring occasionally, until the sugar is dissolved. Bring to a simmer for about 5 minutes, then remove from heat.
2. **Syrup Application:**
   - Once the cake is completely cooled, brush or drizzle the syrup over the cake. This step is optional but adds a nice sweetness and keeps the cake moist.

5. Garnish and Serve:

1. **Garnish:**
   - If desired, dust the top of the cake with powdered sugar and garnish with fresh mint leaves.
2. **Serve:**
   - Slice the cake and enjoy. It's refreshing and light, making it a perfect summer dessert.

Tips:

- **Watermelon:** Ensure the watermelon is well-drained to prevent excess moisture in the cake batter.
- **Texture:** The cake should be light and moist. If the batter seems too thick, you can add a little more milk to reach the desired consistency.
- **Syrup:** The syrup adds extra sweetness and moisture, but you can skip it if you prefer a less sweet cake.

Karpouzopita is a unique and delightful way to enjoy the flavors of watermelon in a cake form. It's a refreshing and light dessert that's perfect for warm weather!

Greek Cheesecake

Ingredients:

For the Crust:

- 1 1/2 cups (150 grams) graham cracker crumbs or digestive biscuit crumbs
- 1/4 cup (50 grams) granulated sugar
- 1/2 cup (115 grams) unsalted butter, melted

For the Filling:

- 8 oz (225 grams) cream cheese, softened
- 1 cup (240 ml) Greek yogurt (full-fat or whole milk)
- 3/4 cup (150 grams) granulated sugar
- 3 large eggs
- 1 teaspoon vanilla extract
- 1 tablespoon all-purpose flour
- Zest of 1 lemon (optional)
- 1 tablespoon lemon juice (optional)

For the Topping (optional):

- Fresh fruit (e.g., berries, sliced strawberries)
- Fruit compote or preserves
- Whipped cream

Instructions:

1. Prepare the Crust:

1. **Preheat Oven:**
   - Preheat your oven to 325°F (160°C). Grease a 9-inch (23 cm) springform pan or line it with parchment paper.
2. **Combine Crust Ingredients:**
   - In a medium bowl, combine the graham cracker crumbs, granulated sugar, and melted butter. Mix until the crumbs are evenly coated and the mixture resembles wet sand.
3. **Press into Pan:**
   - Press the crumb mixture firmly into the bottom of the prepared springform pan to form an even layer.
4. **Bake Crust:**
   - Bake in the preheated oven for 10 minutes. Remove from the oven and let cool while preparing the filling.

2. Prepare the Filling:

1. **Beat Cream Cheese:**
   - In a large bowl, beat the softened cream cheese with an electric mixer until smooth and creamy.
2. **Add Sugar and Yogurt:**
   - Gradually add the granulated sugar and continue to beat until fully combined. Then, add the Greek yogurt and mix until smooth.
3. **Add Eggs and Flavorings:**
   - Beat in the eggs one at a time, making sure each egg is fully incorporated before adding the next. Stir in the vanilla extract, all-purpose flour, lemon zest, and lemon juice if using. Mix until just combined.

3. Bake the Cheesecake:

1. **Pour Filling:**
   - Pour the cheesecake filling over the cooled crust in the springform pan. Smooth the top with a spatula.
2. **Bake:**
   - Bake in the preheated oven for 45-55 minutes, or until the edges are set and the center is slightly jiggly. The cheesecake will firm up as it cools.
3. **Cool:**
   - Turn off the oven and let the cheesecake cool in the oven with the door slightly ajar for about 1 hour. This helps prevent cracking.
4. **Chill:**
   - Remove the cheesecake from the oven and refrigerate for at least 4 hours, or overnight, to fully set.

4. Add Topping and Serve:

1. **Prepare Topping:**
   - If desired, top the cheesecake with fresh fruit, fruit compote, or whipped cream before serving.
2. **Serve:**
   - Carefully remove the cheesecake from the springform pan. Slice and serve chilled.

Tips:

- **Texture:** To prevent cracks, avoid overmixing the batter and ensure that the cheesecake is not overbaked.
- **Water Bath:** For an even smoother texture, you can bake the cheesecake in a water bath. Wrap the outside of the springform pan with aluminum foil to prevent leaks, then place it in a larger pan filled with hot water.

- **Flavor Variations:** You can add other flavorings such as vanilla bean paste or citrus zest for additional flavor.

Greek Cheesecake is a rich and creamy dessert that combines the best of traditional cheesecake with the unique tanginess of Greek yogurt. Enjoy this delightful treat!

Pine Nut Cake

Ingredients:

For the Cake:

- 1 cup (150 grams) pine nuts, toasted
- 1 cup (200 grams) granulated sugar
- 1/2 cup (115 grams) unsalted butter, softened
- 3 large eggs
- 1 cup (120 grams) all-purpose flour
- 1 teaspoon baking powder
- 1/4 teaspoon salt
- 1/2 cup (120 ml) milk
- 1 teaspoon vanilla extract
- Zest of 1 lemon (optional)

For the Syrup (optional):

- 1/2 cup (100 grams) granulated sugar
- 1/4 cup (60 ml) water
- 1 tablespoon lemon juice
- 1 tablespoon honey

For Garnish (optional):

- Additional toasted pine nuts
- Powdered sugar

Instructions:

1. Prepare the Pine Nuts:

1. **Toast Pine Nuts:**
   - In a dry skillet over medium heat, toast the pine nuts until they are golden brown and fragrant, stirring frequently to prevent burning. Remove from heat and set aside.

2. Make the Cake Batter:

1. **Preheat Oven:**
   - Preheat your oven to 350°F (175°C). Grease and flour an 8-inch (20 cm) round cake pan or line it with parchment paper.
2. **Cream Butter and Sugar:**

- In a large bowl, cream together the softened butter and granulated sugar until light and fluffy.
3. **Add Eggs:**
    - Beat in the eggs one at a time, ensuring each egg is fully incorporated before adding the next.
4. **Combine Dry Ingredients:**
    - In a separate bowl, whisk together the flour, baking powder, and salt.
5. **Mix Ingredients:**
    - Gradually add the dry ingredients to the butter mixture, alternating with the milk. Begin and end with the dry ingredients. Mix until just combined. Stir in the vanilla extract, lemon zest if using, and half of the toasted pine nuts.

3. Bake the Cake:

1. **Pour Batter:**
    - Pour the batter into the prepared cake pan and smooth the top with a spatula. Sprinkle the remaining toasted pine nuts on top.
2. **Bake:**
    - Bake in the preheated oven for 25-30 minutes, or until a toothpick inserted into the center comes out clean and the cake is golden brown.
3. **Cool:**
    - Allow the cake to cool in the pan for about 10 minutes before transferring it to a wire rack to cool completely.

4. Prepare the Syrup (Optional):

1. **Combine Syrup Ingredients:**
    - In a small saucepan, combine the granulated sugar, water, lemon juice, and honey. Heat over medium heat, stirring occasionally, until the sugar is completely dissolved and the syrup is slightly thickened. Remove from heat and let cool.
2. **Syrup Application:**
    - Once the cake has cooled, brush or drizzle the syrup over the cake to soak it. This step is optional but adds a nice touch of sweetness and moisture.

5. Garnish and Serve:

1. **Garnish:**
    - If desired, dust the top of the cake with powdered sugar and garnish with additional toasted pine nuts.
2. **Serve:**
    - Slice and serve the cake at room temperature. It pairs wonderfully with tea or coffee.

Tips:

- **Texture:** Ensure the pine nuts are evenly toasted and finely chopped for a better texture.

- **Flavor Variations:** You can add a pinch of ground cinnamon or cardamom to the batter for additional flavor.
- **Syrup:** The syrup helps keep the cake moist, but you can skip this step if you prefer a less sweet cake.

Pine Nut Cake is a rich and satisfying dessert with a distinctive nutty flavor that's sure to impress. Enjoy this elegant treat with your favorite beverage!

Chocolate Greek Truffles

Ingredients:

- 8 oz (225 grams) semisweet or bittersweet chocolate, finely chopped
- 1/2 cup (120 ml) heavy cream
- 1/2 cup (120 grams) Greek yogurt (full-fat or whole milk)
- 2 tablespoons unsalted butter
- 1 teaspoon vanilla extract
- Pinch of salt
- Cocoa powder, finely chopped nuts, or shredded coconut for rolling (optional)

Instructions:

1. Melt the Chocolate:

1. **Heat Cream:**
   - In a small saucepan, heat the heavy cream over medium heat until it just starts to simmer. Do not let it boil.
2. **Combine with Chocolate:**
   - Place the finely chopped chocolate in a heatproof bowl. Pour the hot cream over the chocolate and let it sit for about 2 minutes to allow the chocolate to melt.
3. **Stir Until Smooth:**
   - Gently stir the chocolate and cream mixture until completely smooth and the chocolate is fully melted.

2. Add Yogurt and Flavorings:

1. **Incorporate Greek Yogurt:**
   - Stir in the Greek yogurt, unsalted butter, vanilla extract, and a pinch of salt. Mix until the mixture is smooth and well combined.
2. **Chill the Mixture:**
   - Refrigerate the mixture for about 1-2 hours, or until it is firm enough to handle. The mixture should be scoopable and manageable for forming into truffles.

3. Form the Truffles:

1. **Prepare Rolling Ingredients:**
   - If desired, place cocoa powder, finely chopped nuts, or shredded coconut in separate small bowls for rolling the truffles.
2. **Scoop and Roll:**
   - Using a small cookie scoop or a spoon, scoop out small amounts of the chilled chocolate mixture and roll them into balls using your hands. If the mixture is too

sticky, you can lightly coat your hands with cocoa powder or use a melon baller to shape the truffles.

3. **Roll in Coating:**
    - Roll each truffle in the cocoa powder, chopped nuts, or shredded coconut to coat. Place the coated truffles on a baking sheet lined with parchment paper.

4. Chill and Serve:

1. **Chill Truffles:**
    - Once all the truffles are coated, refrigerate them for about 30 minutes to set and firm up.
2. **Serve:**
    - Serve the truffles chilled or at room temperature. Store any leftovers in an airtight container in the refrigerator for up to 1 week.

Tips:

- **Chocolate Quality:** Use high-quality chocolate for the best flavor. You can choose semisweet, bittersweet, or even dark chocolate depending on your preference.
- **Greek Yogurt:** Ensure the Greek yogurt is thick and full-fat for the creamiest texture.
- **Coatings:** Experiment with different coatings like crushed nuts, sea salt, or even a light dusting of powdered sugar for variety.

Chocolate Greek Truffles are a rich and creamy indulgence, perfect for special occasions or as a delightful homemade gift. Enjoy making and savoring these delicious treats!

Greek Apple Cake

Ingredients:

For the Cake:

- 1 1/2 cups (180 grams) all-purpose flour
- 1 teaspoon baking powder
- 1/2 teaspoon baking soda
- 1/4 teaspoon salt
- 1 teaspoon ground cinnamon
- 1/2 teaspoon ground nutmeg
- 1/2 cup (115 grams) unsalted butter, softened
- 3/4 cup (150 grams) granulated sugar
- 2 large eggs
- 1/2 cup (120 ml) plain Greek yogurt
- 1 teaspoon vanilla extract
- 2 cups (about 3 medium) apples, peeled, cored, and diced (Granny Smith or Honeycrisp work well)
- 1/2 cup (60 grams) chopped walnuts or pecans (optional)

For the Topping (optional):

- 1/4 cup (50 grams) granulated sugar
- 1 teaspoon ground cinnamon
- 1/4 cup (25 grams) chopped nuts

Instructions:

1. Prepare the Oven and Pan:

1. **Preheat Oven:**
   - Preheat your oven to 350°F (175°C). Grease and flour a 9-inch (23 cm) round cake pan or line it with parchment paper.

2. Prepare the Cake Batter:

1. **Combine Dry Ingredients:**
   - In a medium bowl, whisk together the flour, baking powder, baking soda, salt, cinnamon, and nutmeg.
2. **Cream Butter and Sugar:**
   - In a large bowl, cream together the softened butter and granulated sugar until light and fluffy.
3. **Add Eggs:**

    - Beat in the eggs one at a time, making sure each egg is fully incorporated before adding the next.
4. **Mix in Yogurt and Vanilla:**
    - Stir in the Greek yogurt and vanilla extract until well combined.
5. **Add Dry Ingredients:**
    - Gradually add the dry ingredients to the wet ingredients, mixing just until combined.
6. **Fold in Apples and Nuts:**
    - Gently fold in the diced apples and chopped nuts (if using) until evenly distributed throughout the batter.

3. Bake the Cake:

1. **Pour Batter:**
    - Pour the batter into the prepared cake pan and smooth the top with a spatula.
2. **Prepare Topping:**
    - If using, mix together the granulated sugar, ground cinnamon, and chopped nuts in a small bowl. Sprinkle this mixture evenly over the top of the cake batter.
3. **Bake:**
    - Bake in the preheated oven for 35-45 minutes, or until a toothpick inserted into the center comes out clean and the cake is golden brown.
4. **Cool:**
    - Allow the cake to cool in the pan for about 10 minutes before transferring it to a wire rack to cool completely.

4. Serve:

1. **Slice and Enjoy:**
    - Slice the cake and serve. It's delicious on its own or with a dollop of Greek yogurt or a drizzle of honey.

Tips:

- **Apples:** Choose a firm apple variety that holds up well during baking. Granny Smith or Honeycrisp are excellent choices.
- **Texture:** The Greek yogurt adds moisture and a subtle tang. Ensure it's plain and not flavored.
- **Nuts:** If you prefer, you can skip the nuts or replace them with your favorite type.

Greek Apple Cake is a wonderfully moist and flavorful dessert that brings together the comforting flavors of apples and spices. It's perfect for enjoying with a cup of tea or coffee. Enjoy!

Greek Berry Tart

Ingredients:

For the Crust:

- 1 1/2 cups (180 grams) all-purpose flour
- 1/4 cup (50 grams) granulated sugar
- 1/2 teaspoon salt
- 1/2 cup (115 grams) unsalted butter, chilled and cubed
- 1 large egg yolk
- 1-2 tablespoons ice water

For the Filling:

- 1 cup (240 ml) heavy cream
- 1/2 cup (120 grams) plain Greek yogurt (full-fat or whole milk)
- 1/2 cup (100 grams) granulated sugar
- 1 teaspoon vanilla extract
- 2 tablespoons all-purpose flour or cornstarch

For the Berry Topping:

- 2 cups mixed berries (e.g., strawberries, blueberries, raspberries, blackberries)
- 1/4 cup (50 grams) granulated sugar
- 1 tablespoon lemon juice
- 1 tablespoon cornstarch (optional, for thickening)

For Garnish (optional):

- Fresh mint leaves
- Powdered sugar

Instructions:

1. Prepare the Crust:

1. **Preheat Oven:**
   - Preheat your oven to 350°F (175°C). Grease and flour a 9-inch (23 cm) tart pan or line it with parchment paper.
2. **Mix Dry Ingredients:**
   - In a large bowl, combine the flour, granulated sugar, and salt.
3. **Cut in Butter:**

- Add the chilled, cubed butter to the flour mixture. Use a pastry cutter or your fingers to work the butter into the flour until the mixture resembles coarse crumbs.
4. **Add Egg Yolk:**
    - Stir in the egg yolk until the mixture starts to come together. If the dough is too dry, add ice water one tablespoon at a time until it holds together.
5. **Press into Pan:**
    - Press the dough evenly into the bottom and up the sides of the prepared tart pan. Prick the bottom of the crust with a fork to prevent bubbling.
6. **Blind Bake:**
    - Place the crust in the preheated oven and bake for about 15 minutes, or until lightly golden. Let it cool while you prepare the filling.

2. Prepare the Filling:

1. **Mix Filling Ingredients:**
    - In a medium bowl, whisk together the heavy cream, Greek yogurt, granulated sugar, vanilla extract, and flour or cornstarch until smooth and combined.
2. **Fill the Crust:**
    - Pour the filling into the cooled tart crust and smooth the top with a spatula.
3. **Bake:**
    - Bake in the preheated oven for 20-25 minutes, or until the filling is set and the top is lightly golden. Allow the tart to cool completely before adding the berries.

3. Prepare the Berry Topping:

1. **Cook Berries (Optional):**
    - If you want to make a berry compote, combine the mixed berries, granulated sugar, lemon juice, and cornstarch in a saucepan. Cook over medium heat, stirring frequently, until the berries have softened and the mixture has thickened slightly. Allow to cool before topping the tart.
2. **Fresh Berries:**
    - For a simpler topping, just wash and prepare the fresh berries.

4. Assemble and Serve:

1. **Top the Tart:**
    - Once the tart is completely cooled, spread or arrange the berry topping over the filling. If using fresh berries, you can arrange them in a decorative pattern on top.
2. **Garnish:**
    - Garnish with fresh mint leaves and a light dusting of powdered sugar if desired.
3. **Serve:**
    - Slice and serve the tart. It's delightful on its own or with a dollop of whipped cream or a scoop of vanilla ice cream.

Tips:

- **Crust:** If the crust is too crumbly, it may need a bit more ice water. If it's too sticky, add a bit more flour.
- **Filling:** The filling should be smooth and creamy. Make sure to bake it until fully set.
- **Berry Topping:** Feel free to use any combination of berries or adjust the sweetness according to your taste.

Greek Berry Tart combines a crisp, buttery crust with a creamy filling and fresh, flavorful berries. It's a beautiful and delicious dessert that's perfect for any occasion!

Greek Fig Cake

Ingredients:

For the Cake:

- 1 1/2 cups (225 grams) dried figs, chopped
- 1 cup (240 ml) water
- 1/2 cup (115 grams) unsalted butter, softened
- 1 cup (200 grams) granulated sugar
- 2 large eggs
- 1 teaspoon vanilla extract
- 1 1/2 cups (180 grams) all-purpose flour
- 1 teaspoon baking powder
- 1/2 teaspoon baking soda
- 1/4 teaspoon salt
- 1 teaspoon ground cinnamon
- 1/2 teaspoon ground nutmeg
- 1/2 cup (60 grams) chopped walnuts or pecans (optional)

For the Glaze (optional):

- 1/2 cup (120 ml) water
- 1/2 cup (100 grams) granulated sugar
- 1 teaspoon vanilla extract

Instructions:

1. Prepare the Figs:

1. **Simmer Figs:**
   - In a small saucepan, bring the water to a boil. Add the chopped figs and reduce the heat. Simmer for about 5-7 minutes, or until the figs are soft and the liquid has slightly reduced. Allow to cool.

2. Prepare the Cake Batter:

1. **Preheat Oven:**
   - Preheat your oven to 350°F (175°C). Grease and flour a 9-inch (23 cm) round cake pan or line it with parchment paper.
2. **Cream Butter and Sugar:**
   - In a large bowl, cream together the softened butter and granulated sugar until light and fluffy.
3. **Add Eggs and Vanilla:**

- Beat in the eggs one at a time, making sure each egg is fully incorporated before adding the next. Stir in the vanilla extract.
4. **Combine Dry Ingredients:**
   - In another bowl, whisk together the flour, baking powder, baking soda, salt, cinnamon, and nutmeg.
5. **Mix Ingredients:**
   - Gradually add the dry ingredients to the wet ingredients, mixing just until combined. Fold in the cooled fig mixture and chopped nuts (if using).

3. Bake the Cake:

1. **Pour Batter:**
   - Pour the batter into the prepared cake pan and smooth the top with a spatula.
2. **Bake:**
   - Bake in the preheated oven for 35-45 minutes, or until a toothpick inserted into the center comes out clean and the cake is golden brown.
3. **Cool:**
   - Allow the cake to cool in the pan for about 10 minutes before transferring it to a wire rack to cool completely.

4. Prepare the Glaze (Optional):

1. **Combine Glaze Ingredients:**
   - In a small saucepan, combine the water and granulated sugar. Heat over medium heat, stirring occasionally, until the sugar is completely dissolved and the mixture is slightly thickened. Remove from heat and stir in the vanilla extract.
2. **Glaze the Cake:**
   - Brush or drizzle the glaze over the cooled cake for added sweetness and shine.

5. Serve:

1. **Slice and Enjoy:**
   - Slice the cake and serve. It's delicious on its own or with a dollop of Greek yogurt or a scoop of vanilla ice cream.

Tips:

- **Figs:** Ensure the figs are well-simmered to make them soft and easier to mix into the batter. If using fresh figs, make sure they are ripe and sweet.
- **Texture:** The cake should be moist and flavorful with a nice crumb. If the batter is too thick, you can add a bit more water to loosen it up.
- **Nuts:** Nuts add a nice texture and flavor, but you can omit them if you prefer a nut-free cake.

Greek Fig Cake is a delicious and wholesome dessert that combines the rich flavors of figs with warm spices and a hint of sweetness. It's perfect for enjoying with a cup of tea or coffee!

Phyllo Nut Rolls

Ingredients:

For the Nut Filling:

- 1 1/2 cups (150 grams) walnuts, almonds, or pistachios (or a combination), finely chopped
- 1/2 cup (100 grams) granulated sugar
- 1 teaspoon ground cinnamon
- 1/4 teaspoon ground cloves (optional)
- 1/4 cup (50 grams) unsalted butter, melted

For the Phyllo Dough:

- 1 package (16 ounces or 450 grams) phyllo dough, thawed (about 20 sheets)
- 1/2 cup (115 grams) unsalted butter, melted (for brushing)
- Powdered sugar (for dusting)

For the Syrup:

- 1 cup (200 grams) granulated sugar
- 1 cup (240 ml) water
- 1/2 cup (120 ml) honey
- 1 teaspoon vanilla extract
- 1 cinnamon stick

Instructions:

1. Prepare the Nut Filling:

1. **Mix Ingredients:**
   - In a medium bowl, combine the finely chopped nuts, granulated sugar, ground cinnamon, and ground cloves (if using). Mix well.
2. **Add Butter:**
   - Stir in the melted butter until the nut mixture is well combined and slightly moist.

2. Prepare the Phyllo Dough:

1. **Preheat Oven:**
   - Preheat your oven to 350°F (175°C). Line a baking sheet with parchment paper or lightly grease it.
2. **Prepare Phyllo Sheets:**
   - Carefully unroll the phyllo dough and cover it with a damp cloth to prevent it from drying out. Place one sheet of phyllo dough on a clean work surface and brush it

lightly with melted butter. Layer another sheet of phyllo on top and brush again. Repeat this process until you have 4-6 layers of phyllo.

3. Assemble the Rolls:

1. **Spread Filling:**
   - Evenly spread a portion of the nut mixture along one edge of the stacked phyllo sheets, leaving about 1 inch (2.5 cm) from the edge.
2. **Roll Up:**
   - Carefully roll the phyllo dough over the nut filling, forming a tight log. Place the roll seam-side down on the prepared baking sheet. Repeat with the remaining phyllo sheets and filling.
3. **Brush with Butter:**
   - Brush the top of each roll with melted butter.

4. Bake the Rolls:

1. **Bake:**
   - Bake in the preheated oven for 20-25 minutes, or until the phyllo is golden brown and crispy.
2. **Cool:**
   - Allow the rolls to cool on a wire rack while you prepare the syrup.

5. Prepare the Syrup:

1. **Combine Syrup Ingredients:**
   - In a saucepan, combine the granulated sugar, water, honey, vanilla extract, and cinnamon stick. Bring to a boil, then reduce heat and simmer for 10 minutes until the syrup thickens slightly.
2. **Cool Syrup:**
   - Remove from heat and let the syrup cool to room temperature.

6. Assemble and Serve:

1. **Drizzle Syrup:**
   - Once the phyllo nut rolls have cooled slightly, drizzle or brush the cooled syrup over the rolls. Allow the syrup to soak into the rolls for about 30 minutes before serving.
2. **Dust with Powdered Sugar:**
   - Before serving, dust the rolls with powdered sugar if desired.
3. **Serve:**
   - Slice the rolls into pieces and enjoy!

Tips:

- **Phyllo Dough:** Keep the phyllo dough covered with a damp cloth while working to prevent it from drying out and becoming brittle.
- **Nuts:** Use your favorite nuts or a mix for different flavors and textures. Ensure they are finely chopped for a consistent filling.
- **Syrup:** The syrup adds sweetness and moisture to the rolls, making them even more delicious.

Phyllo Nut Rolls are a deliciously sweet and crispy treat that showcases the rich flavors of nuts and honey. They make a wonderful dessert for special occasions or a sweet addition to any meal. Enjoy!

Greek Chocolate Soufflé

Ingredients:

- 2 tablespoons unsalted butter, plus extra for greasing the ramekins
- 1/2 cup (100 grams) granulated sugar, plus extra for coating the ramekins
- 4 ounces (115 grams) bittersweet or semisweet chocolate, chopped
- 3 large eggs, separated
- 1/4 cup (60 grams) Greek yogurt (full-fat or whole milk)
- 1 teaspoon vanilla extract
- 1/4 teaspoon cream of tartar
- A pinch of salt
- Powdered sugar, for dusting (optional)

Instructions:

1. Prepare the Ramekins:

1. **Preheat Oven:**
   - Preheat your oven to 375°F (190°C).
2. **Grease Ramekins:**
   - Butter the insides of 4 ramekins (6-ounce size works well) and dust them with granulated sugar. This helps the soufflé rise evenly and prevents sticking.

2. Melt the Chocolate:

1. **Melt Chocolate:**
   - In a heatproof bowl over a pot of simmering water (double boiler method), melt the chopped chocolate, stirring until smooth. Alternatively, you can melt the chocolate in the microwave in 20-second intervals, stirring between each interval. Let it cool slightly.

3. Prepare the Soufflé Base:

1. **Combine Ingredients:**
   - In a large bowl, whisk together the egg yolks, Greek yogurt, vanilla extract, and melted chocolate until well combined.

4. Beat Egg Whites:

1. **Whisk Egg Whites:**
   - In a separate clean bowl, whisk the egg whites with a pinch of salt and the cream of tartar until soft peaks form.
2. **Add Sugar:**

- Gradually add the granulated sugar to the egg whites while continuing to whisk until stiff, glossy peaks form.

5. Fold Ingredients Together:

1. **Combine:**
   - Gently fold a small amount of the beaten egg whites into the chocolate mixture to lighten it. Then, fold in the remaining egg whites carefully until just combined. Be gentle to maintain the airy texture.

6. Bake the Soufflés:

1. **Pour Batter:**
   - Divide the soufflé batter evenly among the prepared ramekins.
2. **Bake:**
   - Bake in the preheated oven for 12-15 minutes, or until the soufflés have risen and the tops are set but still slightly soft in the center.

7. Serve:

1. **Dust with Powdered Sugar:**
   - If desired, dust the tops of the soufflés with powdered sugar before serving.
2. **Serve Immediately:**
   - Soufflés are best enjoyed right away, while they are still warm and puffed up. Serve with a dollop of whipped cream or a scoop of vanilla ice cream if desired.

Tips:

- **Preparation:** Make sure all your utensils and bowls are clean and free from any grease when whipping egg whites. Even a small amount of grease can prevent the egg whites from whipping properly.
- **Chocolate:** Use high-quality chocolate for the best flavor. Bittersweet or semisweet chocolate works well.
- **Timing:** Soufflés should be served immediately after baking, as they will start to deflate once they cool.

Greek Chocolate Soufflé is a rich and impressive dessert that combines the depth of chocolate with the lightness of a soufflé. It's a wonderful treat for special occasions or a sophisticated ending to a meal. Enjoy!

Greek Pecan Pie

Ingredients:

For the Crust:

- 1 1/2 cups (180 grams) all-purpose flour
- 1/4 cup (50 grams) granulated sugar
- 1/4 teaspoon salt
- 1/2 cup (115 grams) unsalted butter, chilled and cubed
- 1 large egg yolk
- 1-2 tablespoons ice water (as needed)

For the Filling:

- 1 cup (240 ml) light corn syrup or honey (for a Greek touch)
- 1 cup (200 grams) granulated sugar
- 1/2 cup (115 grams) unsalted butter, melted
- 3 large eggs
- 1 teaspoon vanilla extract
- 1/4 teaspoon salt
- 1 1/2 cups (150 grams) pecan halves
- 1/2 cup (50 grams) finely chopped walnuts or almonds (optional, for added texture)

Instructions:

1. Prepare the Crust:

1. **Preheat Oven:**
   - Preheat your oven to 350°F (175°C).
2. **Mix Dry Ingredients:**
   - In a large bowl, combine the flour, granulated sugar, and salt.
3. **Cut in Butter:**
   - Add the chilled, cubed butter to the flour mixture. Use a pastry cutter or your fingers to work the butter into the flour until the mixture resembles coarse crumbs.
4. **Add Egg Yolk:**
   - Stir in the egg yolk until the dough starts to come together. If the dough is too dry, add ice water one tablespoon at a time until it holds together.
5. **Chill Dough:**
   - Gather the dough into a disk, wrap it in plastic wrap, and refrigerate for at least 30 minutes.
6. **Roll Out Dough:**

- On a lightly floured surface, roll out the dough to fit a 9-inch (23 cm) pie dish. Transfer the dough to the pie dish and trim any excess. Prick the bottom with a fork.
7. **Pre-bake Crust (Optional):**
   - If you prefer a crisper crust, you can pre-bake it for about 10 minutes before adding the filling. Simply line the crust with parchment paper and fill with pie weights or dried beans. Bake, then remove weights and parchment.

2. Prepare the Filling:

1. **Mix Filling Ingredients:**
   - In a large bowl, whisk together the corn syrup or honey, granulated sugar, melted butter, eggs, vanilla extract, and salt until well combined.
2. **Add Nuts:**
   - Stir in the pecan halves and finely chopped walnuts or almonds (if using).

3. Assemble and Bake:

1. **Pour Filling:**
   - Pour the filling into the prepared pie crust, spreading it evenly.
2. **Bake:**
   - Bake in the preheated oven for 50-60 minutes, or until the filling is set and the top is golden brown. A knife inserted into the center should come out mostly clean, though it may still be slightly jiggly.
3. **Cool:**
   - Allow the pie to cool completely on a wire rack before slicing. The filling will firm up as it cools.

4. Serve:

1. **Slice and Enjoy:**
   - Serve the pie at room temperature or slightly warmed. It's delicious on its own or with a scoop of vanilla ice cream or a dollop of whipped cream.

Tips:

- **Honey vs. Corn Syrup:** Using honey gives the pie a unique Greek touch with added depth of flavor. If you prefer a more traditional taste, you can use light corn syrup.
- **Crust:** Make sure to chill the dough thoroughly to avoid shrinkage and ensure a tender crust.
- **Nuts:** Adjust the amount of nuts to your preference, and consider lightly toasting them for added flavor.

Greek Pecan Pie combines the classic richness of pecan pie with the distinctive sweetness of honey and a hint of Greek influence. It's a delightful dessert that's sure to impress your guests! Enjoy!

Printed in the USA
CPSIA information can be obtained
at www.ICGtesting.com
LVHW080241161024
793857LV00010B/282

9 798330 408498